Camera Techniques
in Archaeology

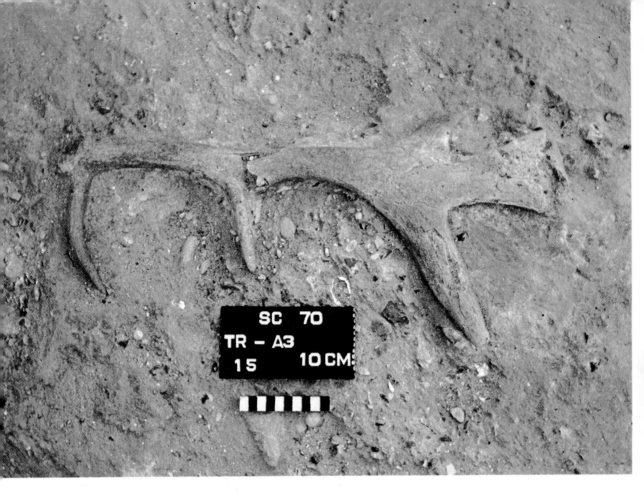

Dr. Waechter, Institute of Archaeology, Excavations at Swanscombe

Colour is the answer to the problem set by these Pleistocene bones in a river gravel deposit, where little contrast would be seen in monochrome. Photographed on Kodachrome film.

Camera Techniques in Archaeology

With 118 photographs and 5 line drawings

V. M. Conlon, I.B.P.I.

Department of Photography,
Institute of Archaeology
in the University of London

John Baker · London

First published 1973
by John Baker (Publishers) Limited
4, 5 and 6 Soho Square, London W1V 6AD

© 1973 Vera M. Conlon

ISBN 0 212 98422 5

Printed in Great Britain by
Clarke, Doble & Brendon Ltd.,
Plymouth

Contents

Illustrations

COLOUR FRONTISPIECE

Pleistocene bones in a river gravel deposit

BLACK AND WHITE PHOTOGRAPHS
(following page 102)

66a, b & c Line drawing, map with red lines to be eliminated, and map with red detail lines eliminated

67a, b, c, d, e & f Examples of screens from books and newspapers, at various magnifications

DIAGRAMS

Acknowledgements

I wish to acknowledge and thank Dr Ian Cornwall, Institute of Archaeology, University of London, for his valuable help in the preparation of this book. Also Susan Johnson, my secretary, who showed such patience in typing the manuscript.

I am grateful to the following for permitting me to use and take photographs of objects in their charge and for allowing me to publish these: the British Museum, the British Museum (Natural History), the Victoria and Albert Museum, the Guildhall Museum, University College London, Mr D. Sturdy, Mr Peter Marsden, Mr Harvey Sheldon, Sir Max Mallowan and Sir Mortimer Wheeler. Also to the Focal Press for permission to reproduce diagrams from the *Ilford Manual of Photography*.

Foreword

by Professor W. F. Grimes, CBE, DLitt, FSA, FMA,
Director of the Institute of Archaeology, University of London

Mrs Conlon has kindly invited me to write a foreword for her book. I do so gladly; for this is my opportunity to express publicly thanks to her, on behalf of the Institute of Archaeology and I am sure also of many archaeologists and others (by no means all of them students at the Institute), for all that she has done to instruct and advise them in the mysteries of her craft over the last twenty-five years.

Any who will read the first *Annual Reports* of the Institute in 1937–8 will become aware of the importance which the founders attached to technical training, recognising as they did its basic value in the collection, recording and treatment of archaeological evidence in general. Here, as in other respects, pioneering work was done. On the photographic side it was by a stroke of genius that (Sir) Mortimer Wheeler drew the late M. B. Cookson to the Institute. The powerful combination of brilliant excavator and dedicated photographer led to standards of visual presentation, particularly in the field, which all since have striven to achieve.

For a variety of reasons, internal and external, Mrs Conlon's contribution to the work of the Institute has been that of a teacher rather than of an expedition photographer. But it is a contribution which in its significant aspects is entirely her own, both in the quality of her teaching and particularly in her assiduous pursuit of new ways of applying photographic techniques to archaeology and archaeological conservation. This book is therefore essentially a practical book. It is the outcome of the author's experience in meeting the needs of people who will not become professional photographers, but will be required to be their own photographers in much of what they do, or at the least must be in a position to understand and appreciate what the camera can do to help them. As a hopeful 'point-and-press' operator of long standing, I have read the text very much to my own advantage; for one thing I appreciate better than I did my colleague's unconcealed surprise at the relative rarity of the occasions when I run into disaster. But while I have been glad to act in a small way as aider and abettor, in this matter I am beyond human aid. *Camera Techniques in Archaeology* should have been written fifty years ago; and thinking back to the trials and tribulations of my photographic youth I can only envy those (of any age) who now have this *vade mecum* to their hand.

W. F. Grimes

Institute of Archaeology,
University of London.

xii

Introduction

Archaeological photography is only one of many specialist branches of the hobby, craft or profession of general photography. It is governed by the same physical and chemical laws, uses equipment and materials primarily designed for general purposes and is subject to the same limitations and practical compromises as any other kind of photographic operation.

It differs from the practice of other branches only in that its subjects, whether in the field or in the studio, present particular difficulties as well as advantages to the practitioner and in that its aims are concentrated on the production of dispassionate factual records rather than pleasing illustrations of them. This is not to say that composition and design are to be disregarded. Just as neatness and cleanliness in excavation are essential, not for themselves alone, but for the clear display without irrelevancies of the field evidence on which archaeological conclusions are based, so the careful planning, preparation and execution of the photographs is an important element in ensuring that they present the facts they are to illustrate as strikingly and vividly, as well as accurately as possible.

To these ends a body of experience has been built up over the last 30 years by specialist archaeological photographers as to suitable equipment, materials, techniques and contrivances to achieve the required high standard of results even under sometimes adverse conditions, with limited time and resources often falling far short of an ideal.

Since experience takes years to acquire and life is short, it is incumbent on anyone who has gained some special experience to set it down in writing for the benefit of those who have not had that opportunity but wish to proceed in the same direction. Thus we progress by building on the foundations laid by our predecessors, adding to them the products of our own experience.

This book, then, is designed to introduce practical instructions on photography, especially as applied to archaeological subjects, to students, amateurs and practising photographers alike who may wish to turn their interests and skills to this particular field. At the same time, not to confine information to mere cookery recipes to be slavishly followed, some explanation of the theory underlying the practice is included, so that readers may adapt their procedures to the demands of particular cases with certain confidence that their approach is sensible and may be attended by some degree of success. For this reason it is to be hoped that the book will appeal as well to workers in other fields who may request accurate photographic records of their special materials—one thinks particularly of geologists, geographers, naturalists of every persuasion, field-workers in general who nevertheless may need in addition to use photographic techniques in the laboratory or at home.

Chapter one – Cameras

THE FIELD CAMERA

On grounds of bulk and weight, both of the camera and its accessories, the classical equipment of the professional, the field camera, is now somewhat out of favour with archaeologists and others working outdoors. It must be admitted, nevertheless, that, for certain purposes and subjects, there is no more flexible equipment: indeed for architectural subjects, where precise work is required, its many movements and universal adaptability make it quite indispensable for obtaining correct perspective.

For the archaeologist it is probably the best camera of all when working on a site for any extended period, when its drawbacks of size and weight are more than outweighed by the added convenience which it gives in tight corners and the ability to correct by eye awkward optical distortions on the ground glass screen before making any exposure.

Old models of field camera, such as the Lancaster, Thornton Pickard and Sanderson, provided with all the necessary movements, in sizes from half-plate to quarter-plate, may still be had for a few pounds. There is, of course, plenty of more modern equipment, based on the old designs, but with later improvements. The Kodak Specialist, the Sinar, the Speed Graphic and the MPP—cameras for the specialist who must have the very best—may easily cost £200 or so.

The big advantage of the field-type camera is the way in which the sensitive material is carried in separate double-darkslides, so that exposed cut-film or plates may be developed directly after exposure to ensure that the picture is a success: if not the shot is easily repeated forthwith. This is essential when the site is producing important and irreplaceable material, which may have soon to be destroyed to reach lower levels on the excavation. If subjects have been photographed on roll-film and this is not developed until some time later, it will be too late to remedy mistakes. The field camera will, of course, take a roll-film back

1

adaptor, if required, and this is useful for making a travel-record or for occasional colour-shots. The advantage of being able to see the subject on the focusing-screen is retained even with the roll-film back and of course all the corrective movements are still available if needed. These are:

(1) The *reversible back*, enabling one to take pictures with the long side of the plate either vertical or horizontal.

(2) *Extensible bellows* which allow the lens-panel to be advanced much beyond the normal near-focus point of the standard lens. In conjunction with lenses of suitable focal length (see p. 14), this makes possible reproduction of the subject at actual size on the negative, or even at some degree of magnification, if required.

(3) The *tilting back* enables correction to be made for otherwise exaggeratedly-converging verticals in an architectural subject, for instance, and for ensuring even focus over the whole plate in such oblique-view situations.

(4) The *slightly extensible back* (with its own bellows) gives even greater extension between lens and screen than the extensible bellows alone and, in addition, allows for an even greater degree of tilt. The *back-focusing* facility thus provided enables maximum sharpness to be obtained at the last moment without altering the distance between lens and subject.

(5) A *rising front* permits an even higher point, such as the summit of a nearby spire or mountain-peak, to be included in the picture without distortion.

(6) The *tilting front* provides for extreme obliquity of view in the vertical direction. In this case it is necessary to use the back to tilt the plate correspondingly in order to ensure over-all correct focus.

(7) *Lateral (cross front) movement* of the lens-panel is useful for centring the subject on the plate, where space for moving the whole camera is restricted (for instance close up to one wall of an excavation-trench).

(8) The *lens-panel* itself enables several lenses of different focal lengths to be fitted as required, by the use of appropriate adaptor-rings which compensate for the varying diameters of the lens-fittings.

(9) *Film-sheaths.* In most dark-slides designed to carry plates, sheet-film may be substituted by the use of metal film-sheaths which hold the film flat and are loaded in just the same way as plates.

The 5"×4"-sized field-camera is recommended as being the most convenient for general purposes. When packed with all its accessories, its weight is not excessive. The size permits enlargements to be made up to a size of 20"×30" without loss of definition.

Two additional methods of loading are available, both for the field- and hand- or stand-cameras:

ROLL-FILM BACK

This is a fitting designed to substitute roll-film at any time for the more usual plate, cut-film or film-pack.

(1) Loaded, the film is led from the unexposed spool across the front of the carrier, which holds the emulsion in the focal plane, and so on to the empty spool. A light-tight sliding cover as in a dark slide, protects the loaded film in front and is withdrawn only for an exposure. The roll-film back may thus be fitted for single exposures only, and then be removed until it is again required.

(2) As in fixed-back cameras, a window in the roll-film back displays the number of the frame next to be exposed.

THE HAND- OR STAND-CAMERA (Technical camera)

This is the ideal substitute for the field-camera in situations where the weight and bulk of the latter are important disadvantages. It retains some of the corrective movements which are a principal feature of the field-camera and, like this, may be adapted to take single plate- or film-holders and, if films are available, film packs or a roll-film back.

There are many different types available and the following list of useful features may be of some help in making a selection:

(1) A *ground-glass focusing back*, which fits into the position occupied by the dark slide.

(2) A *roll-film back*, most generally useful for making a series of exposures in relatively quick succession (Plate 1).

(3) *Extensible bellows*, with double or triple extension, enabling the lens panel to be run out on to a guiding rail, where it may be locked in positions far beyond the normal near-focus limit of the lens. For close-up, or even magnified, subjects.

(4) *The lens-panel* may have the lens in a fixed mount, but, in some cameras, the lens is removable so that any other may be substituted. Because lenses of focal length different from the standard may have mounts of different diameters, ring-adaptors are obtainable which enable them to be screwed into the lens-panel. If this is not the case, combinations of the desired focal length may be arrived at by attaching supplementary lenses of different powers in front of the standard lens (Lenses, p. 16).

(5) A *rising front*, operated by a vertical screw-column, will avoid the necessity

to compensate for perspective-errors in the images of very tall subjects, e.g. mountains, trees, towers, steeples.

Cross-front adjustments may, similarly, be provided, actuated by a transverse screw, thus avoiding the necessity for correcting for obliquity of view in the horizontal plane.

(6) *Single plate-holders* sometimes accompany this kind of camera and these may be adapted for sheet film by the use of rigid sheaths, which hold the sheets of film flat and fit into the holders just as glass plates do.

Hand- or stand-cameras come mostly in the sizes $9'' \times 12''$, $5'' \times 4''$ or $4\frac{1}{4}'' \times 3\frac{1}{4}''$. Not many are still made today, but a good one may be bought second-hand for between £12 and £20. When buying, it would be as well to make sure that the bellows are in light-tight condition. If not, they may still be replaced today, though for how long this facility may continue in the future cannot be predicted.

ROLLEIFLEX CAMERAS (and similar types)

These are roll-film twin-lens reflex cameras, giving a square negative $2\frac{1}{4}'' \times 2\frac{1}{4}''$. This size of negative, though small, gives a reasonable prospect of good enlargements, without problems of graininess, if correctly developed. Their compact shape and light weight make them especially suitable for travelling and for photography in the field and on the site. Main features are:

(1) *Twin lenses*, the lower for taking the photograph, the upper for viewing. The lenses are coupled to the focusing mechanism so that the view seen in the ground glass, and its sharpness, is identical with that projected on to the emulsion, save for a minor error of *parallax*. This is due to the two lenses having slightly different viewpoints and is unimportant save in close-up positions, when the centre of the viewed image will be obviously displaced from that of the image on the film by a distance equal to the distance between the optic axes of the two lenses—a matter of 2″ or so. The error can be compensated for by aiming the viewer at a point 2″ higher on the subject than the centre of the desired field, or, indeed, by taking into the field of view a slightly larger area than that absolutely necessary to display the subject fully. Some cameras have an adjustment, based on slightly converging the optic axes of the twin lenses (normally strictly parallel) to correct for parallax errors in close-up.

(2) *Interchangeable lens-panels* are provided with the Mamiyaflex, each having a matched pair of lenses. Different panels accommodate pairs of the different focal lengths required for various subjects.

4

(3) If the standard lenses are permanently fixed, supplementary lenses of different powers may be added in front of them for close-up work (Lenses, p. 16).

(4) *Focusing screen*. The square ground glass is of the same dimensions, exactly, as the eventual negative. It is surrounded by a hood to cut out some extraneous top-light and improve viewing. In bright sunlight, even this is inadequate and for the best results a dark focusing-cloth or a coat over camera and head is recommended. There is a built-in focusing magnifier. 'Super' viewing screens for clearer viewing can be obtained.

MINIATURE 35 MM CAMERAS

This type of camera is suitable for all specialised recording. It is light in weight, even with all its accessory equipment packed for travelling.

There is a wide choice of many kinds, at widely differing prices and with varying capabilities, from the simple 'point-and-press' pattern with the barest minimum of controls and adjustments to the much more expensive through-the-lens reflex with every imaginable refinement and accessory. The versatility of this meticulously-engineered miniature equipment makes it the favourite of most archaeologists.

The following are some of the more important features of the type:

(1) *The single-lens reflex* provides a view of the actual image to be photographed, up to the instant of releasing the shutter to make the exposure. There is no parallax to be allowed for and final adjustment is possible up to the last moment, even on moving objects, to ensure maximum sharpness.

(2) There are two principal forms of viewfinder:

(*a*) The *ground-glass focusing screen*, with hood and built-in magnifier. This is viewed at right angles to the optic axis of the lens and, in the field, suffers, therefore, from some of the same objections as applied to that of the Rolleiflex (p. 4).

(i) In bright conditions the image on the screen tends to be dimmed by extraneous light, especially when the diaphragm (as is necessary in bright light) is stopped down to a small aperture. Shading the screen is recommended (Pre-set lens, p. 19).

(ii) It is hard to find and hold any moving object (especially with the camera held, with the screen vertical, for an upright picture) when looking, not towards it, but across the line of sight of the lens.

(iii) Owing to the image's having to be formed by a single reflection in the mirror behind the lens, though erect to an observer behind the camera, the image

5

is laterally transposed, so that the finding and holding of the object necessitates movements of the camera contrary to those of the image on the screen. Particularly with moving objects, this calls for considerable practice and dexterity.

(iv) This focusing screen is, however, admirably adapted to work with the microscope in a vertical position, for the image may then conveniently be viewed from the side, instead of from some considerable height above the table or bench on which the instrument is standing. In later models, the screen is removable to admit the substitution of the pentaprism.

(b) *The pentaprism viewfinder*. This, sometimes interchangeable with the above focusing screen, is a device which, when the small rear aperture is brought close to one eye, displays an erect, true image, parallel to the plane of the actual picture. The image moves, when sighting on a subject, *with* the camera and the eye, not contrary to it. It is the fitting of choice for field-work and is almost indispensable for objects in motion. Critical focusing may be aided by a split-image device in the centre of the field of view. The pentaprism is, nowadays, often a permanent fixture, since, for most purposes, it has almost completely superseded the focusing-screen. The availability of the latter nevertheless makes for greater flexibility, as in microscope-work, for instance.

(3) A *Standard lens-ring* (either screw-in or with a bayonet catch) allows the use of quickly interchangeable lenses of various focal lengths.

(4) *Extension-tubes* of different lengths are adapted to fit the lens-ring and the bases of the various lenses. By selecting one of suitable length (or adding several together for greater extensions) the standard lens may be used for increasingly close work, even for photo-macrography, when the image is larger than the object itself. Under these circumstances, focusing becomes extremely critical, depth of focus is greatly reduced and special lighting of the object is almost certain to be necessary. The extension-tubes have the same function, in the miniature camera, as the double- or triple-extension bellows in the field camera.

(5) 'Close-up' photographs may be made either by the use of special 'macro' lenses at short working distances or less conventionally by the use of telephoto lenses at greater working distances, the latter being more suitable for photographing shy, living subjects which would be disturbed by any closer approach of the photographer (small birds or, for instance, butterflies, in the field). Similar views would only, otherwise, be obtainable, by using the standard lens (50 mm) with extension tubes. There is, even so, little depth of focus, and the pentaprism is almost indispensable with this combination.

(6) A *bellows-extension*, for close-up work and photo-macrography (magnified

image), using the 50 mm standard lens, locks on to the lens-ring and carries the lens on its far end. This is continuously adjustable over its whole range for the desired close-up or magnification. The extension-tubes achieve the same effect, but in steps. If much work of this kind is contemplated, the bellows are worth their not inconsiderable price and greatly add to the flexibility of the equipment.

(7) *The focal plane shutter* (immediately in front of the film) is indispensable for a camera with exchangeable lenses and with a reflex mirror behind the lens. It permits faster exposures (up to 1/1000th sec.) than the iris-type shutter in the lens-mount which is common in fixed lenses on non-reflex miniatures. These have a separate view-finder.

(8) In the absence of extension-tubes or a bellows extension (4, 5 and 6 above), *supplementary lenses* (p. 16) may be fitted in front of the standard lens to reduce the working distance and give a larger image. They are much less expensive than those accessories and give quite satisfactory results if correctly used. Through-the-lens viewing and focusing obviates the necessity for conversion-tables to adjust the working distance (necessary where there is a separate view-finder).

(9) *The wind-on spool.* In some miniature cameras, the wind-on spool, which draws the film from the cassette, revolves in a counter-clockwise direction (as viewed from the top of the camera-body). In the cassette, the film is reeled clockwise, similarly viewed. The result of this is that, in winding on, the film is bent round the spool, emulsion outwards, in a direction opposite to the original bend which it received in the cassette. This may cause difficulties in handling the unrolled film during processing in the darkroom, and is to be avoided. Many models roll the film on to the wind-on spool in the same clockwise direction as in the cassette. For practical reasons, this system is to be preferred.

(10) The principal disadvantage of the miniature types of camera is the fixed lens-panel, which allows for no movements to compensate for perspective distortion in close-up. This is especially noticeable in the case of architectural subjects, or, indeed, any, such as excavation-trenches, in which parallel straight lines receding from the foreground are prominent features. With the 50 mm lens in use perspective errors may be minimised by taking the picture from a greater distance, necessarily with some loss of scale and perhaps of architectural detail. Close-ups of buildings, if absolutely necessary, require a wide-angle lens for minimum distortion of perspective. It is, also, as well to avoid, as far as possible, views in which widely-spaced receding parallels are unnecessarily obvious—e.g. sides of a façade at the very edges of the field of view, with the camera tilted steeply upwards to take in the summit of a building. Satisfactory reproduction of fine

detail may be assured by the use of a telephoto lens from some greater distance or by making several exposures from appropriate viewpoints to cover the subject in stages.

Similar considerations apply to human subjects in close-up. Arms and legs extended towards the camera, even long noses in full-face close-ups of the head, may appear to be grossly and comically distorted. The effect may generally be avoided by choosing a different viewpoint or by posing the subject more nearly in one plane parallel to the negative, or by retreating to some little distance. For true-profile views of skulls, for instance, a telephoto lens with the camera at the other end of the room gives a picture free from distortion. The consequent loss of scale may be restored, if necessary, by subsequent enlargement from the negative.

THE POLAROID CAMERA

This is most valuable in a situation where normal negative processing is impossible and an instant-record print is essential.

Various models are obtainable at different prices; some to take pictures in black and white, others in colour.

The camera is simple to use. It includes a built-in light meter and either a synchronised flash or a fitting for a separate flash.

After the exposure is made the print is automatically processed in the camera, so that the result is available within a few seconds. Full operating instructions are given with the various models.

In general only a single print is produced and one disadvantage of the process is that there is no negative from which further prints or enlargements can be made. This can be remedied by making, at leisure, a copy negative from the print while it is still in good condition. In this way a permanent, easily reproducible, record is obtained. As is so often the case in rapid processing, fading or staining of the original may occur after some time.

However, one type of film (Polaroid Negative/Positive) is available, from which a negative is recoverable.

THE CINÉ-CAMERA

At one time the cost of ciné equipment—camera, projector, film—and of processing, discouraged archaeologists from using this excellent method of recording the progress of an excavation from start to finish. Nowadays it is within the means of most and the moving picture—whether with sound or silent—is an admirable medium for introducing people interested in archaeology to digging methods and

8

the handling of materials and tools. Action will hold and impress an audience where still pictures might fail.

Both 16 mm and 8 mm cameras are suitable for professional work as well as amateur. The former is to be preferred for projection on to a full-sized screen.

The technique for photographing in motion has to be learned and practised. A convincing film sequence, however informal it may appear as a finished article, has to be planned and rehearsed, not only as to the action but also as to camera positions, lighting and timing. This means the writing of a detailed scenario beforehand. Continuity between sequences must be assured and this may call for intervening captions, picture footage or sound-commentary. Cutting and editing are themselves skilled jobs if the pictures are to have their full impact.

From the camera-man's point of view, smooth panning across a scene at a speed such that the audience can take in the essentials as they pass, zooming in on distant detail at a steady rate without shakes, coming back to the wider view without faltering, are indispensable techniques which go far beyond the operation of the still camera and are taken for granted by audiences. They all require practice and judgment.

Loading of most cameras is much the same. It is necessary to understand one's camera thoroughly before attempting to expose film. Having removed the cover, the loaded spool is placed, square hole downwards, on the upper reel-spindle and about 2 feet of film are drawn from it. The film-gate and pressure pad are opened, the film threaded into the lead-in slot and the gate again closed. On pressing the starting-trigger the film is automatically threaded in most cameras. When the loose end reaches the lower, empty spool the movement is stopped and the end is threaded into the slot of the take-up spool. Before closing the camera, a short length is run on to the take-up spool to make sure that the film is moving correctly through the gate and is not torn.

Most cameras have a footage- and frame-counter and this must be set to zero once the film is loaded and before shooting. The speed-controller is then set at 16 frames/second for silent film, at 24 for sound and 32 for moderate slow-motion.

If a single-lens camera is used, the viewfinder accurately frames its field of view. Some have a turret-head, by means of which three or more lenses of different focal lengths may, at choice, be brought into the working position by rotating the turret. The viewfinder provided is adjustable, for the particular lenses fitted, to frame their different fields of view. In most cases (i.e. for distances down to about 6 feet from the camera) the slight parallax error of a few inches, vertical and lateral, of the viewfinder in its normal position may be ignored. For close-up work, however, the finder is mounted at the same height as the working lens (vertical parallax nil) and no more than an inch or two to one side of it. This slight lateral parallax may be compensated for by an adjustment on the finder, whose optic axis is made to converge on that of the lens at the working distance used.

The exposure time is affected by the filming speed. For silent films it will generally be 1/30th sec. at 16 frames per second. The use of a light-meter is recommended and this will give the aperture required in particular conditions for an exposure time of 1/30th second. As the filming-speed is increased for sound-film, the aperture will have to be increased accordingly. As for still photography, the meter will have to be set for the actinic speed of the sensitive material before any reading is taken.

Lenses of various focal lengths can be provided for most cameras. On the whole, a normal 25 mm lens will be most useful, for, when stopped down fully, the depth of focus extends from 4 ft to infinity.

The revolving turret carrying several lenses of different focal lengths has lately been superseded by the zoom-lens, which is continuously variable in focal length, without loss of definition, giving images of varying sizes. This feature greatly speeds operation—there being no need for any pause or gap in the action for lens-changing.

Processing of exposed film by a specialist is strongly recommended.

FILM PROJECTOR

This is as important as the camera for producing satisfactory results.

All projectors nowadays should have sound-equipment, even if it is not invariably used.

Apart from the lamp and minor auxiliary fittings the principle of the projector is very like that of the camera.

The film to be projected is in a reel mounted on the upper arm-support. The lower arm takes the empty take-up reel.

Provisions for threading the film through the gate are similar in most models. One should be perfectly familiar with their operation, having practised in advance with old or blank film, before attempting to thread a valuable and perhaps unique film for showing. Unfamiliarity with the projector or the necessary manipulations may result in a torn film and total loss of some frames.

Driving-speed is varied by a continuous rheostat-control or, more simply, by a setting of fixed speeds for silent or sound operation.

Light-intensity is also sometimes adjustable.

A lens of the correct focal length is required according to the length of throw between projector and screen and the size of the screen.

Different projectors have different arrangements for framing-levers, reversing mechanism and for re-reeling films after projection, and other minor adjustments. One should practise to become entirely familiar with the particular projector used.

Finally, it is worth spending money on a good screen. All the preceding good work will be wasted if the image cannot be seen to full advantage on a clean, brilliant, strictly flat screen of appropriate size. A hung bed-sheet or roughly painted, not too clean, wall are unworthy substitutes for a proper screen, save in circumstances of dire necessity!

Chapter two — Lenses

Whatever the form or refinements of body and shutter-mechanisms, ultimately, in any camera, it is the lens, forming the image on film or plate, that is of supreme importance. Other things being equal—and they are many, including the skill and experience of the operator!—the better the lens, the better the photograph.

The design of photographic (as of other) lenses is a highly-skilled technical operation, the tedious calculations for which the computer has now taken over from human designers.

The desirable qualities of a lens are:

(1) That it should pass the maximum of light from the subject to the sensitive material;

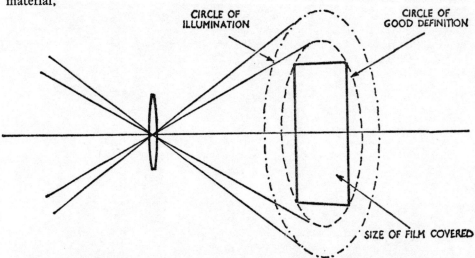

The *Covering Power* of a lens is the area of negative over which it will produce a reasonably sharp image of the object.

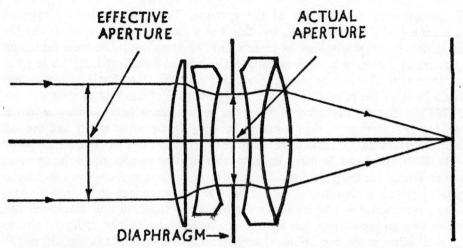

EFFECTIVE APERTURE

ACTUAL APERTURE

DIAPHRAGM→

Relative Aperture
The ratio between the focal length of the lens and the diameter of the aperture.
Thus *f*.8 means an aperture of ⅛ of the focal length.

(2) That it should reproduce a true, undistorted image of the subject with equally good definition (sharpness) at the edges as well as at the centre of the picture (flat field);

(3) That, if it consists of more than one glass element (and some modern lenses are composed of many), there should be as much light passing and as little internally reflected as possible, at the various air/glass interfaces, which might reach the film and degrade the principle image. Modern 'bloomed' lenses do much to achieve this end.

The first two desiderata are, in the nature of things, antagonistic. A simple lens passing light at its maximum aperture is not (because of the aberrations inseparable from spherical surfaces) producing the sharpest image of which it is capable. Stop it down to a smaller aperture, to improve the sharpness of the image, and you inevitably lose a great deal of light and so have to give a longer exposure. Modern lenses with many elements work at large apertures with acceptable definition.

The complications of modern lenses are designed to give the best compromise between these opposed factors—an acceptably sharp image even at the large apertures which make possible reasonably short exposures, even in poor light.

Relative apertures are expressed in '*f*-numbers', the ratio between the focal length

13

of the lens and the diameter of the aperture. Thus, '*f*.8' means an aperture measuring $\frac{1}{8}$ of the focal length, and this was a usual maximum aperture for the meniscus-type of single lens in cameras of 50 years ago. Common maximum apertures of modern miniature anastigmats of 50 mm focal length are *f*.2 or *f*.1·8, i.e. 25 mm or 27·8 mm respectively. At this aperture, the simple meniscus lens would form an image markedly fuzzy over perhaps $\frac{2}{3}$ of the field of view.

This is not to say that modern lenses are by any means perfect—they represent only better compromises than formerly between light-passing ability and over-all sharpness of image. At a maximum aperture of *f*.1·8, so short an exposure (1/500th or 1/1000th sec.) can be given in reasonable lighting conditions in the open air as will 'freeze' the image of a rapidly moving subject and still yield an adequately-exposed negative. Conversely, such a lens will pass enough light from (say) a well-lit stage-scene to give an acceptable picture of static, or only slowly-moving, figures with an exposure of only 1/25th sec. Such results, naturally, depend also on the availability, at the same time, of very fast sensitive materials (Materials, p. 35).

Nevertheless, when (as in most archaeological subjects) there is no call for very short exposures and the lighting, natural or artificial, is sufficient, the maximum sharpness of image, showing the finest detail, is obtained by stopping down a lens, even of advanced design, to minimise its remaining aberrations. Miniature negatives of this kind, if required to illustrate a publication, will certainly have to be enlarged by at least ×4 linear for the half-tone blockmaker, with inevitable, if only slight, loss of quality in the process, so that the better the negative, the better the eventual illustration. For the same reason, ultra fine-grained (if rather slower) negative material is to be recommended for static subjects, the faster films being liable to show 'graininess' on enlargement (Materials, p. 35). Thus, if the subject is inanimate, small apertures, long exposures and slow films give the best archaeological results in the long run using the tripod if need be.

In time, even the best lenses deteriorate, through clouding of the glass elements. As a result, they lose quality, by scattering some of the light they should transmit and pass less to the accurately-focused image. The light so scattered causes slight over-all fogging of the negative, with loss of contrast. Clouded lenses may be re-bloomed, when they once more transmit more light and refract correctly. In practice it is generally only necessary to have the exposed front element treated.

TYPES OF LENSES AND THEIR USES

(1) *Normal focal length.* This lens is used for general purposes. If the desired focal length of a camera-lens for normal purposes is not known, it may be very

approximately estimated by measuring the diagonal of the negative. In miniature film, for instance, the frame measures 25×35 mm, with a diagonal of 42 mm. The normal lens has a focal length of 50 mm. The focal length is, more accurately, the distance between lens and film which gives a sharp image of an object effectively at infinity. It is generally engraved on the bezel of the front lens, along with the maximum aperature, e.g. 1:2·0/50 (*f*.2, 50 mm, focal length).

(2) *Long focal length.* This gives a larger image of distant objects than does the normal lens, but with a narrower field of view. On the other hand, this lens shows less apparent perspective distortion within its proper working range. It should have a focal length sensibly longer than the diagonal of the negative of the camera with which it is to be used.

(3) *Short focal length.* This gives a wider field of view, but an image of reduced size. A lens of focal length equal to the long side of the negative should cover the frame and give an over-all sharp image. If it is too short in focal length for the camera, the edges of the picture will be unsharp while the centre is sharp. This may be corrected, to some extent, as an improvisation, by stopping the lens down hard, but a suitable short-focus lens ought to behave uniformly over the whole field at its rated maximum aperture.

(4) *Wide-angle.* This is a short focal length lens of special design, intended to cover a wide field where working-distance is restricted. Its wide field of view is necessarily accompanied by a reduced size of the image. For the archaeologist or architectural photographer it is invaluable, in the narrow confines of trenches and in tight corners where one cannot stand back to include enough of the subject with the normal lens. It is also valuable to the geologist and topographer, for, despite the loss of scale, it takes in a panoramic view of landscape with a single exposure, often wide enough to be comprehensible, where two or more adjoining views would be necessary with the normal lens.

Wide-angle lenses are made with fields of view from 60° to 180°. Save for very specialised work, those with angles of more than 90° to 100° are not recommended. Maximum permissible apertures are smaller than with longer-focus lenses, in order to give an acceptable image quality. Even so, stopping down a wide-angle lens will tend to increase definition, and is recommended. Stopping down beyond optimum aperture will result in fall-off of definition, owing to the effects of 'diffraction.'

(5) *Telephoto.* This is a lens of exceptionally long focus but with somewhat shorter 'back-focus', for magnifying distant objects, but has a correspondingly narrow field of view. A lens of 150 mm focal length, for instance (3 times that of

15

the normal lens of the 35 mm miniature camera) gives an image 3 times the size—magnification ✕3. At the same time, great care is necessary when using it to avoid camera-shake, for it is relatively heavy and any tremor will be three times magnified in the image. If the camera must be hand-held, for any but a very fast exposure, it is advisable to rest it on, or against, a post, tree-trunk, bridge-parapet or other firm support when exposing. A steady tripod and a cable-release are recommended for the best results.

The telephoto is valuable for photographing inaccessible architectural detail (e.g. vault-bosses in a cathedral) or geological features high up in the face of a cliff or gorge, for example.

Much more powerful (and expensive) telephoto lenses may be obtained for miniature cameras than the 150 mm quoted—so much so, that the camera-body becomes rather an attachment to the lens than *vice versa*! In that case, the lens itself must be supported by the tripod and the camera becomes a mere counter-weight at its rear end.

A lens-hood to prevent internal reflections of extraneous light is recommended for all telephotos. For distant landscapes, a haze-filter (p. 26) is also available.

(6) *Supplementary lenses*, of various focal lengths, may be obtained to alter the focal length of the standard lens. They are fitted on to the front of the camera-lens in the same way as filters. A conversion-table for adjustment of the working distance is supplied with each lens, but its use is unnecessary with reflex or focusing-screen cameras, where the image is directly seen and focused before exposing. On fixed-lens cameras with a separate view-finder, the table enables the new working distance to be found. Supplementary lenses are cheap, but uncorrected for spherical aberration, so that some stopping-down is advisable whenever possible to ensure over-all definition on the negative. Properly used, they give perfectly satisfactory results. They will also change the values of the f-numbers.

(7) *Stops* on a lens to reduce the working aperture have already been mentioned several times. On modern lenses definition is very good even at apertures of $f.2$ and more. In full sunlight, out of doors, however, the use of the maximum aperture is unnecessary and would, with modern fast film, require only a very short—perhaps impossibly short—exposure. Since the definition even of the best lenses is improved by using a small stop, it is evidently best, within practical limits, to reduce the exposure by using a smaller stop than by increasing the shutter-speed. The exception is, of course, when the subject is moving so rapidly that a very short exposure is required to 'freeze' an image that would otherwise have moved perceptibly in the field during the exposure.

The hand-held camera is unlikely to show perceptible shake within 1/100 sec., if ordinary care is taken, though it can, with greater precaution, be so used up to 1/25th sec. The former speed is also quite fast enough to freeze any but a really fast-moving object in the field of view. At 1/100th sec., a suitable stop for (e.g.) Kodachrome II colour-film, photographing an open landscape in full sun between 11 a.m. and 3 p.m. would be *f*.8 or *f*.11—smaller still for the much faster black-and-white film (Materials, p. 36ff).

The scale of stops: *f*.2, *f*.2·8, *f*.4, *f*.5·6, *f*.8, *f*.11, *f*.16, *f*.22 is an inverse logarithmic scale—each larger stop (smaller *f*-number) admitting twice as much light to the emulsion as the preceding.

(8) *Depth of focus.* Depending on the focal length of the lens, its distance from the object and the aperture at which it is being used, focusing to maximum

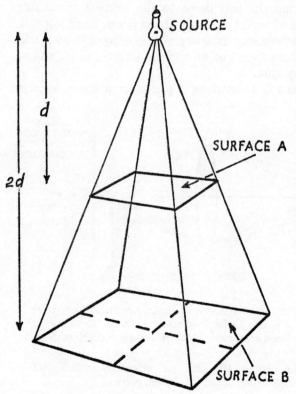

Inverse Square Law of Light
Camera The intensity of illumination on a plate varies inversely with the square of the lens focal length. *Illumination* When an object is illuminated by a light source at a given distance. If the light is moved nearer to or farther from the object, the necessary exposure increases or decreases according to the inverse square law. Twice the distance away $2 \times 2 = 4 = \frac{1}{4}$ strength.

e.g. (1) if the light is at half the former distance the intensity of illumination will be 4 times as great and the exposure required only $\frac{1}{4}$ as long.

(2) if the light is removed to 3 times the distance, the illumination will be only 1/9 of its former intensity and the necessary exposure 9 times as long as before.

sharpness will be more or less critical. In general, a lens of relatively long focal length, used close to its near point of focus and at its widest aperture gives highly critical focusing conditions—only a very small adjustment makes a large difference between an unacceptably fuzzy image and maximum sharpness.

The same lens, at the same working-distance, if stopped down to a small aperture, will prove far less critical, though the image will be reduced in brightness. Stopping down has improved the *depth of field*. When the depth of field is very small, the image of any object having appreciable thickness and varied relief will be unevenly sharp—it will be found impossible to get all of it into focus at once. When one plane is sharply focused, the image of any plane through the object, either nearer to or further from the lens, will be more or less fuzzy.

In all close-up work, therefore, it is advisable: (1) to arrange the viewpoint so that all important features of the subject lie, as far as possible, in a single plane transverse to the lens; (2) to stop the lens down to the smallest practicable aperture, so as to obtain an image of acceptable over-all sharpness. Since stopping down involves loss of light, a relatively long exposure will be necessary and it will probably be advisable to have the camera set up on a tripod or other firm stand to avoid any possible shake during exposure.

(9) *Depth of field*. When a lens is focused on a particular distance, objects

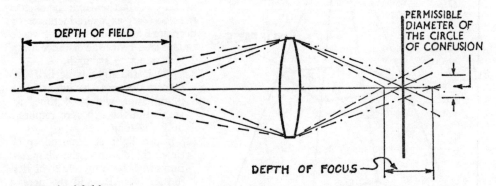

Depth of field
When a lens is focused on an object at a particular distance, objects lying not far beyond and within this distance will also be fairly sharply rendered. The distance between near and far objects which are acceptably sharp is known as depth of field.

Depth of focus
The distance through which the camera lens can be racked backwards and forwards while preserving satisfactory image detail for a given point.

beyond and in front of this distance will also be sharply rendered. The distance between the near and far objects is known as depth of field. A short-focus or wide-angle lens will have a greater depth of field than a long-focus or telephoto. In all cases, stopping down the aperture will bring the acceptable near-point closer to the lens. This will be at the expense of some loss of light and the accompanying necessary longer exposure.

(10) *Lens-hood*. With the sun (or other light-source) more or less behind the camera, the lens is shaded from most unwanted light, but if the subject is between the camera and the main source of light (*contre jour* effect), not only is there some risk of direct 'flaring' of the film by the inclusion of the light-source itself in the field, but the lens is exposed, also, to all kinds of indirect, refracted and reflected light from objects (even atmospheric dust-particles, mist-droplets, etc.) from the general direction of the light-source.

A lens-hood, projecting for some distance in front of the lens, serves to cut out most extraneous light which might cause 'flare' in the image, without in any way encroaching on the field of view. It may with advantage be used at all times in the field, though, when attached, it sometimes interferes with the fitting of filters and supplementary lenses for special purposes. In that case, it may have to be removed. In the absence of a lens-hood, the hand or hat may often be so held during the exposure as to shade the lens from the worst of the extraneous light, without its intruding into the field of view.

SHUTTERS

The shutter is a device for allowing light, focused by the lens, to fall for a pre-arranged period of time on the sensitive emulsion of the film and, when closed, to protect the latter from exposure to any light at all.

(1) *Focal-plane shutter*. This is the type used in most hand, and miniature cameras with interchangeable lenses. As its name suggests, it operates almost in the focal plane, immediately in front of the sensitive face of the film and out of the way of the reflex-mirror, if there is one. It is a double blind, incorporating slits of variable size, and the speed with which the chosen slit traverses the frame to make an exposure is determined by variable spring-loading of the blind mechanism. Available speeds are pre-set on the camera-body. The shutter-release is generally a press-button on the body of the camera, or, if a lens with pre-set aperture-control is fitted (whereby the iris diaphragm closes to the chosen aperture only at the 'first pull' of the shutter-release), the back of the release-button on the lens presses the body-release to set off the shutter once the iris has closed. Speeds up

c   19 to 1/1000th sec. can be obtained with the focal-plane shutter. It is considerably faster than the diaphragm-type (see below).

The focal-plane shutter has two possible slight disadvantages: (1) there may be slight distortion of the image of a fast-moving object. Irrespective of what direction the fast-moving object is travelling in, distortion of one form or another will occur;

(2) the action of pressing the release-button, if careless or too vigorous, may introduce camera-shake at the moment of the exposure. The use of a cable-release prevents this, especially in close-ups or microscope work, when the camera is fixed on a tripod or stand and all vibration must be avoided.

(2) *Diaphragm-shutter.* In many non-removable lens-mounts, the shutter is situated close to the iris diaphragm controlling the aperture. It works, much as does the iris itself, by overlapping leaves of metal which open and close radially. The shutter may be in front of, or behind, the lens, or more usually between the separate glass elements of a compound lens. It is practically silent and vibrationless. The fastest exposure available is no more than 1/750th sec. Speeds are selected by a radial lever on the lens-mount, which is pre-set at the mark indicated. Bulb and time-settings are generally provided and there is a socket for a cable-release as well as the ordinary hand trip-release. The shutter has to be wound up, by means of a lever, for each exposure, in all save miniature cameras, in which it is, nowadays, generally geared to the wind-on movement of the film, this arrangement preventing double exposures.

(3) *Lens-cap for hand-exposures.* The lens-cap, generally provided as a protection for the lens of a studio or field camera, is often used as a shutter for time-exposures of 1 sec. or more. The exposure is timed by counting the seconds, or with a watch or seconds-timer clock for longer times. It is important, in making hand-exposures, to remove the cap and hand smartly, sideways, from the field of view and to bring it back quickly and smoothly when recapping the lens.

(4) *Cable-release.* This has already been mentioned several times in particular contexts. When the camera is hand-held, for short exposures, the body release-button or the trip-release on a diaphragm-shutter may be operated carefully, without fear of shake. When the camera is independently supported on a tripod or other stand, however, and especially for the longer or time exposures, releasing the shutter directly involves a real danger of introducing vibration. By using a cable-release of suitable length, the reaction opposed to the action of pressing the shutter-release is transferred from the operator to the camera itself, and cannot shake it as long as the cable hangs slackly between hand and camera. Its use is

20

also recommended in the field for all longer exposures and invariably when using the telephoto lens or in extreme close-up. In these cases the camera would, in any case, preferably be mounted on the tripod.

(5) *Delayed-action release*. Some miniature cameras are fitted with clockwork-driven delayed-action shutter releases. This allows up to a dozen seconds of time after pressing the trigger for the photographer to appear personally in the picture, to pose along with the rest of a group.

This is not its only use. The delayed action allows the release-button to be pressed directly and the hand to be removed, so that the shutter is automatically opened and closed again without vibration, for a longish or pre-set bulb exposure up to several seconds in length. This makes unnecessary the use of a cable-release when the camera is mounted on its tripod.

The delayed-action gear has to be wound up, generally on the top of the camera body, before selecting the exposure on the same knurled knob. In a particular instance, there is a delay of 12 seconds before the shutter-release is automatically tripped.

Chapter three — Filters and accessories

A filter is a sheet, generally a disc, of glass or other transparent substance (e.g. coloured gelatine) which is placed in the optical axis, filling the aperture of the camera-lens, with the object of modifying the quality of the light reaching the sensitive material. Such modification consists in the absorption by the filter of a chosen band, or bands, of wavelengths in, or adjacent to, the visible spectrum. The filter should not affect transmission of any other part of the spectrum, nor, of course, interfere with image-formation by the lens, so that it should be optically flat.

Glass filters. The colours are provided by clear sheets of dyed gelatine. For protection, these are cemented between thin cover-glasses and so are not easily scratched and, if finger-marked, are easily wiped clean. They are more expensive than bare gelatine, but last indefinitely (apart from some fading of the colour after long use or undue exposure to sun) and so are strongly recommended.

Gelatine filters. These sheets of coloured gelatine are cut to fit interchangeable filter-holders, fitted in front of the lens, or they may be inserted behind the lens. They have to be handled with great care, for they are easily marked and soon become useless if damaged.

Filters are used in photography for several distinct purposes:

(1) To correct the tone-rendering of the panchromatic film, which, though it responds in some degree to all colours, does so unevenly, giving over-emphasis to ultraviolet and blues and under-emphasising the red end of the spectrum. Exactly uniform representation of the whole spectrum is not desirable either, for the human eye is most sensitive to a band in the yellow-green region, so that, to be true to the scene as the eye sees it, the film should also slightly over-emphasise the yellow green. This is achieved by fitting to the lens a pale yellow or yellow-green filter, which absorbs a proportion both of the blue and of the red ends of the spectrum, but passes all the intermediate yellow-green light available.

22

(2) To select and emphasise the contrast (not always appreciable on a mono-chrome negative or print) between differently-coloured parts of the subject, which may, otherwise, have similar or identical tone-values. This is particularly valuable for showing details of stratification in archaeological and geological sections in the field, differentiating between finds, still *in situ*, and their background and so on.

An example will make this clear.

In a section through the earthen rampart of a hill-fort, the buried land-surface on which the rampart-material was piled up displays the profile of the soil formed at that surface before the construction. The rampart-material is yellowish-brown, a stony loam, while the upper part (A-horizon) of the ancient soil is a relatively stoneless loam of only very slightly darker tone, but of a distinctly greenish-grey hue, owing to reduction in airless conditions of its iron salts by the decay of the organic matter which it once contained.

Ordinary panchromatic film would probably not record the same degree of contrast as that apparent to the eye, because of the clear distinction to the eye between the *colour* of the buried soil and that of the yellowish rampart make-up.

The difference might be accentuated by using an orange or (more strongly) a red filter. The filter would pass most of the light reflected by the yellowish-brown material, so that it would be rendered as a dark tone on the negative and a light on the eventual print. The greenish buried soil, however, would itself absorb much of the red, orange and yellow fractions of the daylight falling on it and reflect to the camera only the yellow-green to blue-green parts. Most of this band would be absorbed by an orange or red filter, so that, in the end, very little light at all from the buried soil would reach the film. The resultant negative, therefore, would have a very pale image of the buried soil, which, in a print from it, would appear very dark—in marked contrast to the much lighter overlying layers of the rampart make-up.

An observer comparing this print with the original subject would recognise that it somewhat exaggerated the differences in tone between the two parts of the section, but, as an illustration to the eventual excavation report, it would convince the reader of the reality of the colour distinction described in the text.

This is an entirely justifiable proceeding, and is in no way comparable to 'painting the lily' (i.e. retouching the negative or print). This is to introduce an artifact to the photograph—a most immoral procedure and one absolutely forbidden in archaeological photography!

(3) To cut out ultraviolet radiation which is, in particular, diffused by haze in

23

a distant landscape and may slightly fog the whole image of the scene. In the case of mist (liquid droplets suspended in the atmosphere), as opposed to the solid particles of (say) a dust-haze, a band of relatively long wavelengths should be selected to form the image (red, or even infrared—see below) because these longer-wave radiations penetrate water-vapour and are less absorbed than the shorter-wave (blue) end of the spectrum.

Though giving a clearer image of a misty distance, this wavelength selection will upset the colour-balance of the image, by making yellow, green blue and violet areas of the scene very dark on the print and lightening the reds. A red sandstone cliff backed by blue sky would come out as a white cliff against an almost black sky, but, if originally dimmed by mist, with much improved sharpness and detail.

A dark sky produced in this way gives contrast and an air of drama to well-lit architectural features seen against it.

In general, one selects a filter of the *same* colour as the area of the subject to be *lightened* for better contrast on the print. To *darken* any feature, a filter of the colour *complementary* to its natural colour is fitted.

COMPLEMENTARY COLOURS

If the six primary and secondary colours are arranged as sectors of a circle, the colour in each sector will be diametrically opposite to its complementary colour—red opposite blue/green, yellow opposite blue and magenta opposite green (and *vice versa*). A filter of the first colour will pass light of its own colour but absorb and exclude from the camera light of its complementary colour.

Since all filters pass a more or less wide *band* of wavelengths, and more or less absorb the rest, a red filter, for instance, will pass chiefly red, with some violet and orange in lesser intensity. It will absorb most completely in its complementary band, blue-green (cyan). A filter of a paler red will be less selective, a darker more so, but the latter will absorb a larger fraction, and transmit a smaller, of the total light available, than the former.

FILTER FACTOR

Since the function of a filter is to absorb light in some part of the spectrum, it follows that, when it is in use, less light, in total, reaches the film. For correct exposure, therefore, the exposure-time or the aperture must be correspondingly increased. The factor by which the exposure should be increased, using a particular filter, is marked on the filter or its container ($\times 2$ $\times 4$, $\times 10$—or whatever it may

24

be). This factor will depend on what film is used and the colour-temperature (p. 37) of the illumination.

YELLOW FILTER

We have seen the effect of the red filter and have mentioned the function of the yellow or yellow-green in assisting the panchromatic film to give a generally truer tone-rendering of the image as seen by the eye. One effect, in this field, of fitting a yellow filter is to show contrast between the sky (over-emphasised by panchromatic film and so unduly light on the print) and white clouds in it, which, without the filter, would scarcely show at all. The eye distinguishes clearly between a sunlit white cloud and the surrounding blue, but the unaided film does not. Reducing the amount of blue light reaching the film by a pale yellow filter gives something like the true contrast, which, to the eye, resides in difference in colour rather than in tone.

GREEN FILTER

This cuts out magenta light reflected by particular parts of the subject and so darkens them on the print. By passing greens, with some adjacent blue and yellow, it would, for example, lighten patches of vegetation in contrast to the bare ground in a predominantly rusty-coloured desert landscape, or give contrast to the leaves of a climbing plant growing against a red brick wall.

BLUE FILTER

By absorbing yellows strongly and accentuating blues, this exaggerates the tendency already noted of the panchromatic film to over-represent blues, but in poor lighting might be useful to bring out details of blue colour not otherwise in adequate contrast with its background. A *pale* blue may be used in colour photography to give a passable imitation of daylight to a daylight-type colour-film used in artificial (filament-lamp) illumination. It is a last-ditch subterfuge at best! A considerable filter-factor is involved—perhaps $\times 10$.

ORANGE FILTER

This passes both red and yellow wavelengths to some extent, absorbing green, blue and violet. It would show the ripe fruits on an orange tree, for instance, in white on the print, against the almost black, glossy foliage. It is used in the field to accentuate (by lightening in tone) orange and yellow-coloured strata among dark or dirty browns and greens.

ULTRAVIOLET HAZE FILTER

This is widely used in colour photography to reduce the overall blueness of distant landscapes which results from U.V. radiation dispersed by haze and mist. The filter is colourless, so does not affect the standard exposure either in colour or black-and-white photography.

The *U.V. absorbing filter* has a special use in the photography of fluorescent subjects excited by ultraviolet radiation. It cuts out any of the primary radiation reflected by the object, which might swamp the effect of its fluorescence, which, of course, is in the visible wavelengths, not the ultraviolet band. Here the human eye is an unreliable guide, because, though the camera will record them, the operator may be unaware of the presence of such undesirable reflections until he has developed a negative.

INFRARED (I.R.) FILTER

This is used in conjunction with special film sensitive to infrared radiation, which is, like U.V. at one end, beyond the visible range of the spectrum at the other extreme. The filter passes only radiation in the infrared waveband. This band is much less dispersed by mist and water-vapour in the atmosphere than the visible wavelengths and will render a scene apparent to the camera which is invisible, or nearly so, to the operator.

Other uses are the detection of alterations in documents or forgeries in paintings, which may look perfectly acceptable to the eye when photographed in ordinary light, as do the originals, though showing clear tone differences in their response to infrared radiation. By excluding all but the dark red and infrared wavebands, the filter accentuates such differences.

POLARISING FILTER

Since light reflected from a polished non-metallic, or wet, surface at an angle of about 45° tends to be preferentially polarised (vibrating in one plane only), a polarising filter, one which passes light vibrating in a single plane only, can be 'crossed', i.e. orientated at right angles to the vibration plane of the reflected beam. No light from the plane-polarised beam can then get through, though all that vibrating in any other plane does so more or less freely.

Such a filter may be fitted, and adjusted by rotating it, to cut out prominent and unwanted reflections from the field of the subject, which might, otherwise, obscure detail.

This facility is useful when photographing objects behind glass (e.g. in a museum-

26

case, fish through the side of their tank or divers beneath the surface of a sheet of water). Foreground reflections from the intervening surface may thus be eliminated, with great improvement of the picture.

Similarly, in colour-work, reduction of any irrelevant white-light reflections from the subject increases colour intensity appreciably.

Since sky light from a direction at right-angles to the direction of the sun is also appreciably polarised, by reflection from particles in suspension in the atmosphere and gas molecules, the polarising filter may be used to control the apparent brightness of the sky without changing its colour. It is a matter of adjustment to obtain the best effect under the circumstances.

Filters, thus, make available many refinements of rendition and adjustments of what the camera sees. In the case of those affecting visible parts of the spectrum, something of the effect obtainable in the camera may be judged by viewing the subject by eye through the appropriate filter. It must always be remembered, however, that the eye and the sensitive material have somewhat different colour responses and the visible effect of interposing the filter between the eye and the subject will never be exactly that resulting from its use, on the eventual print.

EFFECT OF CONTRAST FILTERS WITH PAN MATERIALS

| Filter | Final (print) tone reproduction of: | | | |
	Blue	Green	Yellow	Red
Deep Red	Very Dark	Dark	Light	Very Light
Deep Green	Dark	Very Light	Light	Very Dark
Deep Blue	Very Light	Dark	Dark	Very Dark
Deep Cyan	Light	Light	Dark	Very Dark
Deep Magenta	Light	Very Dark	Light	Light
Deep Yellow	Very Dark	Light	Very Light	Light

THE LIGHT-METER

This is an essential piece of equipment if consistent results are to be obtained under the most varying conditions. An experienced operator, of course, learns to make a good guess at the correct aperture and exposure time to be allowed for an accustomed subject (say, an open landscape without great lighting contrasts in the immediate foreground) under ordinary conditions (say, full sun within a couple of hours on either side of noon) in view of the speed of the film which he normally uses. For black-and-white photography, in which the latitude of the material compensates for all but gross errors of judgment, and under familiar conditions, such subjective estimates may yield generally satisfactory results. So many are the variables, however—weather conditions, time of day, time of the year in higher latitudes, not to consider differences in subject, speed of negative materials and the range of lens apertures usable under the given conditions—that it is usually advantageous (and economical) to use a light-meter *and to rely upon* its objective assessment of the actual situation.

Some cameras have built-in light-meters. Should one of these fail, it is an advantage to have to hand another meter to give an independent 'second opinion'.

The *photo-electric exposure-meter* is an instrument which measures the intensity of the light received from the subject at the camera position. A photo-electric (selenium or copper-oxide) cell develops a small voltage across its electrodes when excited by incident light. This is led directly to a sensitive galvanometer which records the reading on a numbered scale. The calculator dial is first set so that the figure representing the relative speed of the film in use appears in the index-window. It is there fixed. The movable arrow of the dial is then turned to coincide with the figure given by the galvanometer reading for the light value of the subject, when a range of *f*-numbers and the corresponding exposure times is displayed, any pair of which will give the correct average exposure under the existing lighting conditions. The word 'average' is important. The meter, like a computer, is incapable of independent adjustment to peculiar circumstances, unless these are presented to it in its own limited terms—in other words, it records what it can see: neither less nor more, and does not criticise what it sees in the light of what may be wanted of the scene by the photographer.

If the subject is, for instance, a cliff or archaeological section in shadow, with a strong light from the sky coming in over its summit, a light-meter aimed in that general direction will record a reading including some of this interfering sky light, which will be much higher than that corresponding to the part of the view which it is desired to record. The meter must, then, be shown only so much of the picture as is significant—it must be shielded from extraneous light by a cupped hand, or otherwise, and read when it is receiving only light reflected, however dimly, by the desired detail. The exposure calculated from this reading will be the correct one for the real subject, and if some area of sky does come into the eventual picture, that area will be grossly over-exposed. This will involve no loss, for it was, in any case, irrelevant.

Such precautions are particularly important in reversal colour-work, for the film has very little latitude and will not record the colours of the subject at all accurately unless the exposure chosen for the important part of the scene is very close to the correct one. The film is technically incapable of correctly recording very wide contrasts in lighting in the same scene.

Thus, if the subject is a building in full tropical sun with part in deep shadow, the chances are that, if the well-lit details are correctly exposed (as the meter will prescribe), the dark features will be so shadowed, in contrast, as to be invisible. Conversely, if the exposure is adjusted to record the details in the shadow, the sunny side of the subject will exhibit but a pale, over-exposed, image of its real modelling. The solution is to expose the whole picture on another occasion in diffused sky light. The meter will, in the second case, give the correct figure. Hard shadows and strong high-lights should, in any case, be avoided.

In the case of the immovable object in bright sun which casts black shadows, it would be well to wait to take the photograph until a cloud happens to obscure the sun momentarily. A quick meter-reading, for the transient conditions, would be needed. Should there be no clouds and no other likely opportunity to see the subject under more favourable conditions, two readings—one for the part in full sun and the other for that in shadow—might be taken. An exposure midway between the two extremes should make the best of a bad job—for in an extreme case neither part will be more than *approximately* correctly exposed.

The photo-cell is covered, for bright lighting conditions, by a perforated baffle-plate, which admits only about 1/10th of the available light. This prevents overloading of the photo-cell, which is, however, sensitive enough to read even in very poor light. For this purpose, the baffle is swung away and clipped in its fully-open position. The movement brings into view opposite the galvanometer needle a second scale of light-readings, with a range of only 1/10th of the former at full deflection. These enable exposures (even time- and bulb-exposures of several seconds duration) to be correctly computed. Having used the meter with the cell thus fully exposed, it is important to return the baffle to its normal position before putting the meter away, for the photo-cell may be damaged by overloading if it is next used at full sensitivity in brightly sunlit conditions. For microscope work, where light-intensities are often low, a specially sensitive meter, the SE photo-meter, applied directly to the focusing-screen, is recommended.

FLASH-PHOTOGRAPHY

Since the quality of a photograph depends entirely on there being enough light on the subject, and since there is often not sufficient natural light available for the matter in hand, either in the studio or out of doors—say, for example, in an ill-lit corner of an excavation—if photographic lamps and the electric power to drive them are wanting, a small, portable battery-powered flash-unit will often solve the problem, provided that it has sufficient covering-power.

Flash-bulbs are cheap and may be operated directly from a dry battery. One type is filled with pure aluminium foil or aluminium/magnesium alloy wire, which, when fired, gives a brilliant flash of some milliseconds' (ms) duration with a colour-temperature (3,800°K)* much higher than that of tungsten-filament lamps (ordinary, 2,800°K; photoflood, 3,400°K).

There are three grades of flashbulbs: F (fast), M (medium) and S (slow), of about 20, 30 and 60 ms flash-duration, respectively. S gives by far the best total illumination and the other two are worth consideration only for moving subjects which call for shorter exposures. A fourth grade, FP (focal plane) is slower than any, so that its light-production curve against time has a flattish peak of relatively constant illumination for up to 30 ms, the time taken for the slit of a focal-plane shutter to traverse the frame, at shorter 'instantaneous' exposures. For longer exposures, the S-type flash is completed while the blind is fully open. So, too, for 'bulb' and 'time'-exposures, timing of the flash presents no special problem.

Most modern cameras are fitted with synchronizing electric points for shutter-operation simultaneously with the firing of a flash. Exposures down to 1/50th, 1/25th and 1/10th sec. are respectively practicable for the F, M and S types of flash-bulb.

For static or practically stationary subjects, where the flash is to provide the bulk of the illumination, the camera is set up on a tripod, the shutter opened at 'bulb' (using a cable-release), the flash ignited and the shutter immediately released. The correct exposure is controlled by the stop in conjunction with tables of distance between flash and subject, which determine the intensity of illumination obtained.

Electronic flash. The equipment is expensive at the outset. A miniature type without heavy batteries is available for use in the field. It can be recharged where mains-electricity is available and the tube fires a considerable number of flashes between charges.

Exposures are calculated from a distance-to-subject table supplied with the equipment, which gives the appropriate apertures and shutter-speeds for each working-distance.

* °K = °C + 273.

30

The camera needs special synchronizing-points, except for bulb- and time-exposures. In these cases, with the shutter open, a series of hand-held flashes, perhaps directed on to the subject from several different angles to build up the total exposure, will be required. This technique is especially valuable in caves (and other situations in total darkness) for interesting lighting of complicated, three-dimensional features. Effects may be staged, in advance of the several flashes for the actual exposure, by using hand-lamps or candles strategically placed. The trial light-sources (and, of course, the flashes) if from any position in front of the camera, must not be directly visible to it. If the topography does not offer any suitable natural shield, an artificial one which is inconspicuous must be devised.

Flash-photographs in which the flash originates at or close to the camera position are inevitably flat, shadowless and so relatively featureless and uninteresting—see any newspaper! If the subject is itself flat (e.g. an archaeological or geological section)—well and good. One does not, in that case, *want* shadows of minor or irrelevant irregularities. If, however, it should be a rock engraving, however slightly in three, rather than only two, dimensions, using side-lighting with reflectors to soften shadows, or several flashes, or a combination of all three, will make a more interesting and informative picture. In the case of a shallow engraving, it would be the only possible way of getting a meaningful picture at all!

Exposures and details of the lighting arrangements of all flash-photographs should be noted for further reference. Success in this field is very much a matter of trial and error and the experience, once gained, is very well worth recording.

TRIPOD

A firm stand, free from any suspicion of shake, is essential for time-exposures, or, indeed, for any exposure longer than 1/25th of a second. If a long-focus or telephoto lens is fitted, it is advisable to use a tripod, if conditions permit, in any case for exposures down to 1/100th sec. In the absence of a tripod, or where there is no time to set it up, resting the camera, or the hand holding it, on a fence-rail, against a tree-trunk, car-body (engine switched off!) or any available steady support will lessen the likelihood of perceptible camera-shake, even during longish exposures. This, however, is a makeshift and much less reliable than a firm stand. A cable-release should always be used to release the shutter in any of these circumstances.

(1) A heavy tripod will always be steadier than a light one, but for small cameras a lighter tripod is permissible, if only for its greater portability.

(2) Rigidity of the tripod when set up depends on there being no play in any of the joints—the hinges of the legs as much as in the extensible parts of the legs themselves. Telescopic and jointed legs will wear and become loose with constant use, so that an eye should, from time to time, be kept on the satisfactory condition of these parts.

(3) A vertical pillar, raised and lowered by rack or friction-gear and designed to be firmly clamped in position, is desirable to carry the camera-head. This enables a high viewpoint to be reached, a frequently necessary position when looking downwards into an excavation, thus avoiding undue distortion of the foreground when a short-focus lens is in use.

(4) A tripod should have interchangeable feet—spikes with adequate spuds to prevent undue sinking into soft ground (e.g. loose spoil on a dump) for field-work; rubber-shod feet to avoid slipping on (for instance) the polished floor of a museum. It is as well also to have adjustable safety-chains between the legs, to prevent their collapsing if they should slip when widely spread. For low-placed subjects or points of support for the legs on different levels the legs should be fully adjustable in length.

LOADING-BAG

This is a light-tight bag of heavy fabric with a slide-fastener opening covered by a flap, to enable dark slides, films or developing-tanks to be put into it. It has two sleeves with elastic-fitting cuffs, by which the hands may be inserted to work freely inside it without admitting light.

After a little practice, reloading of slides and even processing of exposed films or plates can easily be carried out in it, in places where no darkroom is available.

The exposed part of a film may be cut off and removed from the camera for quick processing, without sacrificing more than a few frames of the unexposed portion.

Should anything go wrong with the winding on or back of the film in the camera (not unknown if it is carelessly loaded and, for example if a perforation in the film gets torn where it passes over the sprocket), the fault can be detected and rectified on the spot if a loading-bag is carried. Otherwise, the jam may have to wait for nightfall or a return to base—with possible loss of the better part of the day's work.

At a pinch, the principle of the loading bag may be applied by finding the darkest corner available, covering the camera with a thick coat or jacket, weighted down round the edges with rocks and opening it under this by inserting the hands through the sleeves. With luck and good management a minor mechanical fault may be quickly corrected without fogging the film. It is, at the best a clumsy substitute for the real thing and to be recommended only in a crisis. No more lengthy operation than this should even be attempted.

Chapter four – Negative materials

SENSITIVE NEGATIVE MATERIALS (BLACK-AND-WHITE)

The whole process of photography (literally, 'writing with light') depends on the peculiar property possessed by some pale-coloured silver salts: in that, once having been quite briefly exposed to light, they darken on further chemical treatment (development) by reduction to metallic silver. If the light falls on a surface coated with such materials in an ordered pattern, or 'image', on development, a perfect reproduction of the latent (hidden) image is obtained, but in negative—dark where the image was bright and *vice versa*, with all gradations of tone in between. To reverse this, and reproduce the original tones of the image, it is necessary to pass light through the finished negative on to another surface of sensitized material, when, after development of this second image, a 'negative' (positive or print) of the first photographic image is obtained.

This process has remained fundamentally unchanged since its invention, though the materials and apparatus with which it is nowadays carried out have been improved beyond recognition. In particular, the sensitivity of the materials to very short exposures of the lens-image has been increased enormously and a high degree of acceptable reproduction, even with very varying degrees of exposure ('latitude') is available, compensating for errors on the part of the operator. Even a comparatively uninstructed photographer, therefore, can expect to achieve pictures of adequate quality almost from the outset, merely by observing a few commonsense rules.

The light-sensitive salts are suspended as an uniform emulsion in melted gelatine. The emulsion is mechanically spread evenly on glass plates or coated on to reels of clear cellulose acetate or other transparent plastic film, where it sets and dries. A carefully filtered atmosphere is maintained to prevent blemishes which might arise from dust settling on the still-soft emulsion. The plate or film is provided with a coloured backing which absorbs any light which might be reflected back to

34

the emulsion from the film or glass surface. The entire manufacturing and packing process has to take place in darkness, or, at the most, in a subdued light of a wavelength to which the particular emulsion concerned is not sensitive.

Roll-film and film-packs are devices which make the loading of the unexposed film into the camera easy and convenient, even in daylight, though some shade from direct sun or clear sky light is desirable. The professional who uses plates or cut-film has still to load his dark-slides in the darkroom before going into the field, or to take with him a light-proof changing bag in which the necessary operations may be carried out wherever he may be.

SPEED OF EMULSIONS, 'GRAIN'

The relative sensitivity ('speed') of a photographic emulsion is bound up with the grain-size of the individual particles in it of photo-sensitive salts. Coarser particles give 'faster' emulsions, but a developed image composed of larger crystals of silver, which if greatly enlarged, give a noticeably 'grainy' appearance and a consequent loss of definition. The finer the salt-particles in the emulsion, the 'slower' is the material in its response to the exposure, but the 'grain' is by so much less apparent, even after a high degree of enlargement, therefore the material has greater capacity to reproduce fine detail in the image with high definition.

Though the size of grain may be modified in the process of development, by the use of dilute solutions and relatively low controlled temperatures (see Development, p. 43), where it is possible for other reasons a fine-grained (and so relatively slow) original negative material should preferably be used. Archaeological subjects are generally static and, if a tripod is used (as in most cases it should be) the longish exposures necessary for fine-grain material are no drawback in a situation where the maximum definition is a primary objective. This is especially the case when the camera is of miniature (35×24 mm) format. The small negative will require a considerable degree of subsequent enlargement to yield a print of a size to be viewed adequately without additional magnification.

Comparative emulsion-speeds are expressed on several scales: ASA or Weston are mostly used by manufacturers in English-speaking countries; DIN in Germany. They are easily inter-convertible by the use of published tables. Speeds of monochrome negative materials on ASA/Weston scales range from 50 (slowest) to 1000 (fastest). The faster are inevitably subject to graininess, however developed, and should not be used unless speed of exposure is an essential feature of the kind of photography to be undertaken.

SENSITIVITY OF MATERIALS TO COLOUR AND INVISIBLE RADIATIONS. SPECTRUM

A narrow beam of white light, on passing through a slit and a prism, is broken ('refracted') into a band of 'rainbow'-colours, ranging from dark red through red, orange, yellow, green, blue to violet. This is the visible spectrum, the different colours of which, because of their different wavelengths, are more or less bent in their paths by the prism and so can be seen separated, instead of all together.

The deep red has a wavelength of 740 nanometres* (nm) and the violet of 420 nm. Between these limits lie all of the visible colours.

Photographic emulsions may, however, be sensitive, beyond the range of the human eye, upwards into the infrared (I.R.) and downwards into the ultraviolet (U.V.) wavebands.

SENSITIVITY OF PHOTOGRAPHIC EMULSIONS

Different types of emulsion show different sensitivity to light in the several regions of the visible and invisible spectrum. Their uses for different purposes vary accordingly.

LIGHT SOURCES

Not only do emulsions vary in sensitivity, but so do the actinic ranges of the sources of primary radiation used to illuminate the subject.

In selecting a negative material suitable for a particular purpose, therefore, the spectral character of the available visible illumination—daylight, arc-lamp, tungsten filament lamp, fluorescent tube, mercury-vapour lamp, expendable or electronic

---

* Wavelengths of visible light and of adjacent parts of the electromagnetic spectrum have long been measured in Ångström Units (Å or ÅU).

$$1 \text{ Å} = \frac{1}{10,000,000} \quad (10^{-7}) \text{ of 1 millimetre.}$$

By recent international agreement, Système International (S.I.) Units, based on the metre, multiples $\times$ 1,000 and fractions $\times \frac{1}{1,000}$ thereof, are henceforth to be the only standards of length.

The nanometre (nm), $\frac{1}{1,000,000}$ (10^{-6}) millimetres, will generally, from now on, be used to express light-wavelengths. 1 nm = 10 Å, so the measurement in nm is easily derived from that in Å by dropping one zero.

36

flash—must be taken into consideration, as also its content of invisible radiations, which may likewise affect the sensitive emulsion.

BLUE-SENSITIVE ('NON COLOUR-SENSITIVE') EMULSION

This, the only type of emulsion available to the early photographers, is sensitive only to radiation at the short-wave end of the visible spectrum (down to 400 nm). Beyond this, it is also affected by the near U.V. band (down to 330 nm). Thus, it does not respond even to greens, let alone the yellows and reds of the long-wave end, so that these come out black on the eventual print.

It is of high contrast, if rather slow, and is of use in contexts where colour-rendering in tone is unimportant or unnecessary. Such situations are in the copying of black-and-white subjects, such as documents, line drawings, half-tone illustrations or prints. It is also used in papers for making prints or enlargements from

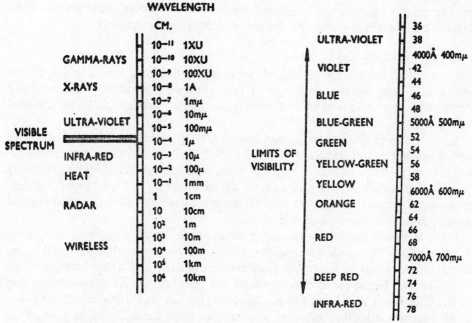

The electromagnetic spectrum   *The visible spectrum expanded*

[The millimicron (mμ) is now called nanometre (nm)]

black-and-white negatives. Many printing papers are made sensitive also to the green part of the spectrum for increased speed.

Owing to its restricted sensitivity, blue-sensitive paper may be processed with a red, orange or green safelight in the darkroom. If it is also green-sensitive, only a recommended safelight should be used.

ORTHOCHROMATIC EMULSION

This is an emulsion made sensitive to longer wavelengths (green), in addition to the blues and U.V., by the addition of a red dye. The name—'correct-colour (rendering)'—is an exaggeration, for the material does *not* respond to orange and red (wavelengths longer than about 590 nm), but nevertheless is hallowed by use, on this understanding. Its high sensitivity in the yellow-green region does, however, correspond with that of the human eye, so that for subjects like landscapes in the temperate zone, where the greens and blues of vegetation predominate, it will give adequate colour-rendering. It will still register red parts of the subject as black on the print—e.g. make a bright-red pillar-box in a street-scene appear to be black! It is therefore unsuitable for many archaeological subjects.

PANCHROMATIC EMULSIONS

These are still further dye-sensitized, up to about 680 nm, taking in the orange and lighter reds, beyond the range of orthochromatic emulsions, and so giving practically true colour-rendering over the whole visible spectrum (Normal Panchromatic).

Some grades of panchromatic film, however, (Hypersensitive Panchromatic) give rather exaggerated emphasis to the red end of their sensitivity-range. This is in order to make them as fast as possible when used in artificial (tungsten filament) light, which is rich in reds and poor in the blue end of the spectrum. They are, thus, *out of balance* in comparison with the eye, as regards all-over sensitivity and so are less suitable for working in daylight.

Since increased sensitivity to colour increases the total amount of light from a given subject to which an emulsion will react, panchromatic films tend to be faster (other things being equal) than orthochromatic, and orthochromatic than blue-sensitive, but speed is also governed, for instance, by the average grain-size of the light-sensitive salts in the emulsion, so this cannot be assumed in all cases.

All panchromatic films must be processed in total darkness, or, at most, with a *very dim* blue-green (about 500 nm) safelight, a wavelength which falls in the band of their minimum sensitivity.

For process-work or copying of diagrams which include coloured as well as black lines, Panchromatic process-film should be used.

Desired variations in colour-sensitivity may be introduced, where panchromatic emulsions are concerned, by the use of appropriate filters (see p. 22).

(see p. 22)

INFRARED EMULSIONS

These are specially sensitized to record invisible radiations, of wavelength longer than 700 nm and up to about 1200 nm. They are used for special purposes, such as the penetration of haze or mist, by which these longer-wave radiations are less scattered than are the visible wavelengths. Since these materials are sensitive also in the blue and U.V. bands, an infrared filter which absorbs completely all the shorter wavelengths must always be used in conjunction with I.R.-sensitive material.

A further point is important: since I.R. radiation is less sharply refracted by the lens than the visible wavelengths, the focal point for such rays will be *behind* the focal plane for the visible colours, for which the lens-focus points of the camera are calculated. For I.R. work, therefore, the lens should be racked slightly forward. The difference is large enough to be important for critical definition, though still small—only about 0·3% to 0·4% of the focal length of the lens. The correct focus will generally have to be found by trial and error, though some modern cameras are marked with an infinity-point for I.R. work.

Infrared-sensitive film is often unavoidably 'grainy'. The effect may be minimised by special slow development technique.

With reference to the recommendation of the use of Kodak Infrared IRER 5″×4″ plates, it should be added here that Kodak have now discontinued this item.

It has been replaced by High-speed Infrared film, Serial No. 4143, in the same 5″×4″ format.

With the 88A filter, aperture f.45 and 2 Photoflood 500-watt lamps, at a distance from the object of about 3 feet, 3–4 secs. exposure will be required.

With misty sun, in daylight, using a 5″×4″ camera and Infrared filter, an aperture of f.45 with an exposure of 1/5 sec. will be found to be satisfactory.

Develop in DG10 R 1–4, for 3 mins. at 68°F.

Successful results were obtained in tests of this film, used as stated.

This extremely fast film must be held in dark-slides of a material suitable for shielding infrared-sensitive film—i.e. non-metallic and non-conducting of heat—otherwise fogging may easily occur.

COLOUR-EMULSIONS

Two kinds are available: the 'reversal'-type, for producing positive colour-transparencies, and the negative-type for making colour-prints on paper.

Reversal film is available in grades balanced on the one hand for use in daylight, and on the other for correct colour-reproduction in artificial (tungsten filament or flash) light. With negative film, adjustments are made by the use of filters. All appropriate instructions for the use of filters, etc. are enclosed with the film. It is important to ensure that the proper type and grade are obtained for the job in hand.

COLOUR-FILM

Emulsions by different makers differ considerably in colour-rendering—one make for instance emphasising the blues while another brings out reds and browns more prominently. In all cases, correct exposure within fairly narrow limits is necessary for satisfactory colour-rendering. It nevertheless remains for the photographer to select the type of emulsion best suited to his subject and the circumstances of the case—for instance it would be preferable to use a more red-sensitive type for distant landscapes in the blue-misty low-contrast subdued lighting of northern Scotland, if an overall preponderance of blues and blue-greens is to be avoided.

DAYLIGHT PHOTOGRAPHY

Colour-photography out of doors, especially at high altitudes, under very clear skies, or with subjects including much reflection from water or snow, may result in a picture tending unnaturally to over-all blueness, with purple or violet in the shadows. The cause is the ultraviolet radiation accompanying the visible colours in the illumination reflected from the subject or diffusing direct into the camera from sky and clouds. Since ultraviolet is invisible to the eye while strongly affecting the sensitive emulsion at the blue end of its range of response, the resulting photograph differs appreciably, by exaggerated blueness, from the general colour of the scene as viewed by the photographer. The cure is simple—an ultra-violet haze-filter fitted before the lens, which absorbs excess ultraviolet while passing all the bands of the visible spectrum unchanged. Since the filter is colourless, no factor for increase of exposure is necessary. A lens-hood which shades the lens from extraneous oblique irradiation without infringing on the field of view provides further necessary protection from glare in the visible wavebands. The exposure-meter gives useful guidance in such a case, but, being sensitive as is the emulsion to ultraviolet, must not be relied on implicitly as it will prescribe an exposure shorter than that required to record the visible colours most truly. Experience, based on careful notes taken on comparable past occasions, will suggest appropriate modification of the exposure as given by the meter in a particular case.

For pits and trenches on an excavation, which, with oblique direct sunlight, would partly be in deep shadow, the deep blue effect of ultraviolet would be particularly obtrusive. A high sun, preferably veiled by continuous thin cloud, giving a more uniform diffused top-lighting, is what is required, so that the slanting light of early morning or late afternoon should be avoided for that reason in such subjects. Passing clouds in a clear sky will also introduce variations in lighting hard to gauge. Not only so, but the actual quality of light early or late in the day differs from that of midday. In the middle of the day it will tend to blueness with violet shadows if the weather is clear. In the early morning or evening the light will be yellower or redder, with more purple in the shadows.

Where it is desired to reproduce detail in an unavoidably shaded area (for instance the north-facing wall of a trench), a reading must be taken of the subject with the meter carefully screened against extraneous light from above and ahead. Allowance must be made for a lens-aperture somewhat reduced for purposes of critical focusing, but not stopped right down, for the necessary long exposure required with a very small aperture may result in some change in colour of a colour-film. The makers recommend the shortest practicable exposure time for the best results. As ever, choice of a particular combination of aperture and exposure is something of a compromise, dictated by the prevailing circumstances.

In more southern latitudes colour photography by daylight presents fewer problems as lighting conditions during the day are often less variable, though the relentless high southern sun with its accompanying hard (if short) shadows may call for special devices to mitigate excessive contrasts in archaeological subjects.

ARTIFICIAL LIGHT

Special types of colour-emulsion are made which are corrected for the much lower colour temperatures of artificial light sources, as compared with daylight. Alternatively a daylight-type film may be used in conjunction with a pale blue 'tungsten' filter, as prescribed by the makers, which cuts out some of the excessive red and yellow wavelengths in artificial illumination but at some cost in increased exposure-time.

Colour pictures of objects in the studio are not difficult to obtain successfully under conditions where even lighting can be arranged to prevent unwanted shadows and excessive contrasts in the subject. General views of interiors, however, where much special lighting cannot be installed, may raise considerable problems. Acceptable results may be achieved only by trials with various combinations of the available lights, both artificial and natural, sometimes both together. Preliminary exposures should be processed and criticised for any possible improvements before the final run. At the same time one should be warned against the dangers of combining light sources of differing colour temperature.

As in all colour-work, reasonably even illumination of all important detail should be sought, for colour-emulsions have only very slight latitude, if a fairly true rendering of the actual colour is expected. Thus, the range between highlights and shadows must be kept within strict limits or there will be areas of the resulting picture unacceptably over-exposed as well as some unduly dark, along with the better-reproduced intervening bracket of tones. Awkward shadows may be relieved by a fill-in flash.

Indeed, if the real subject is not always available, such trials may be carried out elsewhere on a colourable mock-up, the devices approved in this way being carefully noted for duplication on 'the day'.

True colour is controlled in all emulsions—negative or positive, daylight or artificial light types—by exposures, filters and processing. Some films may be developed at home by the formulae specified by their manufacturers. Kodachrome, a specialised film with several distinct emulsion layers which are individually dyed during processing can only be developed by the makers.

When considering a choice of film-emulsions and suitable lighting, composition of the picture should not be overlooked. Even factual photography, for the recording of archaeological or scientific materials, need not always be pedestrian and inartistic. A slight change of viewpoint, after due consideration, may often convert a quite ordinary subject into something interesting and even striking.

Chapter five – Processing

DEVELOPMENT

On exposure to an image of varying tone in different areas, the grains of silver halide in a photo-sensitive emulsion absorb radiant energy in proportion to the intensity of the light falling upon each. They thus become potentially susceptible, in different degrees, to attack and alteration by the chemical reagents which will be applied to them to make the latent image visible during the subsequent process of development.

The essential reaction which takes place during development is the reduction of silver halide (pale) to metallic silver (dark). It takes place most rapidly and intensely in those parts of the latent image which have received the most light.

Ideally, none of the unexposed sensitive particles should be reduced, but, in practice, if immersion in the developer is continued for long enough, all will eventually be blackened, so that over-development results, first, in loss of contrast between the desired image and the unexposed parts of the film and, finally, in over-all 'fog' of the negative. Developer concentrations, temperatures and times are therefore normally adjusted to control the degree to which the latent image is developed without allowing unexposed parts of the emulsion to darken perceptibly. The process of development thus allows for a certain flexibility and room for the exercise of skill and ingenuity in modifying the effect of the exposure on the negative by varying the factors governing development—concentration, temperature and time.

Developer solutions, in general, contain, in addition to (1) the developing- or reducing-agent proper, (2) a preservative, which prevents this from being uselessly oxidized by the atmosphere, or by air dissolved in the water used to make up the solution, (3) an accelerator, an alkali or alkaline salt, to provide the optimum pH-conditions for the reduction, and (4) a 'restrainer', which prevents early attack by the reducing-agent on unexposed halide-particles in the emulsion.

Developing-agents are generally more or less complex organic substances, or

43

mixtures of substances, and there is a considerable choice of possibilities, all of which have their special effects. Most developer-solutions, therefore, are nowadays commercially formulated and the accompanying literature describes their particular qualities and gives directions for their correct use.

The principal types are:

(1) *Normal developers*. These are for general use and if to be used in the tropics (where in the absence of refrigeration, developing temperatures are unavoidably high) they have added a hardener, to prevent undue swelling of the emulsion-gelatine during development. Instructions for normal development of negative materials in dish or tank, and for printing-papers, accompany the package.

(2) *Fine-grain developers*. These are suitable especially for small and miniature negatives, in which the grain-size must be kept to a minimum, to avoid loss of quality on subsequent enlargement. Because fine-grain developers are necessarily slow in action, the negative tends to be 'soft' (with somewhat reduced contrast), a feature which may be corrected by enlarging on to a fairly 'contrasty' paper.

(3) *Contrast developers*. If the original subject was lacking in contrast, or the negative was likely, for any reason, to have been much under- or over-exposed, this developer will strengthen the contrast in the image.

(4) *High-contrast developers* are designed for use with the special high-contrast negative materials used in process-work.

(5) *Kodak D76 developer*. This is a fine-grain developer for use with a wide range of types of negative materials as well as infrared-sensitive materials, which are unavoidably 'grainy'. I would recommend, even so, dilution to one part in three (1 : 3) instead of 1 : 1, as recommended in the instructions.

(6) *Reversal developer* is used in combination with certain other chemical processes for producing a positive image direct from the exposed negative, as in making lantern-slides. Instructions are provided with the package.

Replenishers are packs of developer-reagents for adding to tank-developers in order to maintain their concentration and activity and to prevent their becoming weakened or exhausted by use.

DEVELOPING EQUIPMENT

(1) *Tanks*. Deep developing-tanks of adequate dimensions are adaptable to the development of plates or flat films of any size. These are hung on edge in the solution by rustless frame-hangers, which rest on rails along the sides of the tank. A systematic quick lifting and lowering of the hangers provides sufficient agitation to ensure that the developer in contact with the emulsion surface is replaced with a

fresh sample before it becomes exhausted, with the attendant possibilities of arrested, or uneven, development. Replenishers (see above) are used to keep the solution up to rated strength. When covered, the tank is light-proof, so that other work can go on in full light while development is in progress.

(2) *Dishes*, of all necessary sizes, are useful for developing a trial-negative or for using a special developer not generally required. This method calls for undivided attention and constant agitation of the small quantity of solution for satisfactory results. A dark-room, with or without a safelight appropriate to the grade of film being developed, is necessary.

(3) *Roll-film tanks*. While roll-films may also be dish-developed, for routine-work tank development of films saves time and manipulation. The tank is provided with a spiral spool to hold a length of film with all its surfaces free. Spools may be adjustable to take films of different widths. By the use of a loading-bag (p. 32) the film may be loaded into the spool in daylight and, once covered with its light-tight lid, the tank may be taken out and development and fixing proceed in full light. Reagent-solutions are introduced and drained through a light-trapped central hole and agitation of the contents is assured by occasional movement of the rod protruding from this hole. Inspection of the developing image is not possible, so the duration of development must be determined by the use of time/temperature tables. The tank does not permit special treatment during development of individual frames of an entire film—all receive an equal dose. One or more separate frames cut from a film may be individually treated.

FIXING

Once the latent image has been developed (i.e. formed in metallic silver) in the emulsion, the next essential operation is to remove all unexposed and unreduced silver halides and so to clear the emulsion in the unexposed areas ('fixing'). The fixing solution is sodium thiosulphate (less correctly, 'hyposulphate'—whence the traditional abbreviation 'hypo') which is a solvent for the now-unwanted unreduced silver salts. By removal of these, the unexposed parts of the emulsion become finally insensitive to light—hence, 'fixed'.

It is important that the fixing-bath should be at the same temperature as the developer (whatever that may be). If it should be markedly colder, the expanded gelatine emulsion suddenly shrinks and cockles into 'reticulations', which give a mottled effect on printing or enlargement. Acid hypo (e.g. Kodak 'Unifix') is generally used and this both neutralises the remaining alkalinity of the developer and at the same time limits softening of the emulsion, which is liable, otherwise, to swell unduly during the final washing process, which, to be complete, is necessarily prolonged.

Hypo-eliminator. This is recommended for use when the complete washing of films is difficult because of shortage of water (as may sometimes be the case in field-darkrooms in the Near East or other arid lands).

PRINTING

Even the best negative will only give a good print if this operation is properly carried out. Since the print is the final product, all the preceding care with the negative is nullified unless the best possible print is obtained.

The positive impression of the negative is made, either by passing light to the paper through the negative, this being with its emulsion surface in contact with that of the printing paper (contact-printing), or by enlargement—projecting a (generally magnified) image of the negative on to the paper through an enlarger.

Some experience is required to assess the qualities of a negative and to select the proper grade of printing paper to give the best result.

Bromide papers are made in various grades, to give differences in degree of contrast to the print, whereby minor, or unavoidable, shortcomings in the negative may be corrected in printing.

(1) A 'thin' (under-exposed) negative is printed on 'contrasty' or 'extra-contrasty' paper.

(2) A well-exposed, normal negative—medium paper.

(3) An over-contrasty negative, with extreme high-lights and shadows—'soft' or 'extra-soft' paper.

(4) Film is used for printing a positive transparency from the negative, as in making lantern-slides. This is generally a matter of *reduction* from the negative-format to that of the standard slide. Miniatures may be printed by contact from miniature negatives.

Printing-papers are made with glossy, matt or rough finishes to the emulsion surface. For our purposes (ultimately, possible reproduction for publication) only glossy prints need be considered, for they give the maximum definition and tonal range. The other kinds may be suitable for 'soft' effects in portraiture or art-work, but would be scorned by a process-block-maker!

DEVELOPMENT OF PRINTS

Makers of printing-papers recommend suitable developers and these are provided with time-and-temperature tables to ensure correct processing. Individual development of prints in dishes is the usual practice—or no more than two or three together in a large dish for the more expert operator. They must be vigorously agitated throughout development and fixing to avoid uneven processing or staining. Some latitude is permissible in development without loss of quality. A print slightly over-exposed may be a trifle under-developed, and *vice versa*, but first trial-prints should always be given strict time-and-temperature treatment and any desired adjustments be made in subsequent trial pieces, once a nearly-correct exposure has been obtained.

FIXING

The fixing solution for papers is preferably of acid-hypo, generally of only half (20%) the concentration used for negatives (40%). Ten minutes' fixing-time is recommended, and should not be exceeded, for over-fixing may result in loss of contrast and staining of the paper. At tropical temperatures, an added hardener of chrome-alum is also recommended, at the rate of 12.5 g./lit.

WASHING

Thorough washing is all-important for prints required as permanent records. If insufficiently washed in running water to remove last traces of reagents, they may, in time, fade or become discoloured. If there is no running water or even water by the bucketful is precious, as in dry countries, hypo-eliminator should be used (see above, p. 46). Thorough re-washing once the home base is reached is worth while for maximum permanency of the prints.

CONTACT-PRINTING IN THE FIELD

The simplest printing equipment is the frame, which has a glass front, like a picture-frame, and a removable spring-loaded back which, when in position, keeps the printing-paper in firm contact with the back of the negative.

The negative is first placed on the glass, emulsion-side upwards and the paper next laid on it, emulsion-side downwards. The back having been inserted and clipped firmly, the face of the frame is exposed, generally to the light of an ordinary tungsten-filament lamp, for an appropriate exposure-time. Daylight may be used for the exposure, but, if so, 'gaslight' paper, or a specially formulated slow-emulsion paper is recommended.

If the operator has no idea of the correct exposure to be given, a test-print may first be made, in several strips, each differently exposed, to find by trial and error the most suitable exposure. Holding the printing-frame at a constant distance from the lamp, an opaque card is held covering its face and this is then slid away in (say) four successive stages at 2-second intervals. The first-exposed strip has then had 8 secs exposure, the middle two 6 and 4 secs respectively and the last only 2 seconds. On development by strict time-temperature rules, it will be seen whether the best exposure-time lies within this bracket or not. If not, it will be immediately apparent from the result in which direction further tests will have to be made. If so, another test between, say 6 secs and 2 secs, by 1-sec intervals will, after development, show within 1 second what the correct exposure should be. Since time is here the variable being investigated, the distance between frame and lamp during all test-exposures must be kept constant within narrow limits, or the results will not be comparable. With varying distance, the inverse-square law will apply: halve the distance and the light-intensity will be multiplied by 4: double it, and the light received will now fall to $\frac{1}{4}$ of its first value.

ENLARGING

The enlarger is, in effect, a projection-lantern, throwing a magnified image of the negative-transparency on to the printing-paper to form the positive print which will be the finished photograph. As with any kind of printing, second-rate equipment or poor workmanship in this department will make of no account all the care and skill that may previously have been engaged in the production of a fine negative.

(1) An enlarger should be chosen, bearing always in mind the kind of work that it may be expected to do.

(2) For the enlargement of miniature negatives, lighting by condenser is best. A condenser is a large double lens which collects rays diverging at wide angles from the lamp and concentrates them into a beam which converges into the projection lens and is so arranged that it covers the negative area uniformly.

(3) Opal lamps provide an evenly-diffused light which ensures even cover of the whole area of larger negatives in a diffuser-enlarger (see below). Condenser-enlargers are also designed for negatives even of large formats.

(4) Just as, in the camera, the lens is the most important part, so, in the enlarger, it must be of equal quality if it is to do justice to the negative image formed by the camera-lens. The enlarger-lens must have the covering-power to give an image sharp all over, even at large magnifications.

(5) The negative-carrier has to be well masked all round, so that no stray chink of light may show round the edges of the carrier. There are two types of carrier: one with glasses, the other without. Where the negative lies on a glass plate and

48

is covered by another it is easy to ensure its flatness. The glasses, however, are liable to collect dust. Even though first carefully cleaned, if a single grain of dust remains on the glass, it may be sharply focused in the plane of the negative, be magnified with it and its image be projected on to the print, marring the negative-image with a black spot, which will print white.

The glassless carrier has a frame into which the negative fits without other support. It is not so easily assured that it is perfectly flat, but there are no glasses to collect dust or show minute scratches and any dust particles remaining on the negative will not be held so closely to its surface, and so are likely to be out of focus and less obtrusive. There are only two surfaces—those of the negative—to be kept clean, instead of six! An anti-static cloth should be used for the purpose.

(6) In a diffuser-enlarger, the lamp gives a brilliant illumination over the whole surface even of a large negative. The negative must be well masked in the plane of the carrier and, of course, the lens must give a sharp focus over the whole area of the projected image.

ENLARGERS (p. 48)

Enlargers may often be purchased at quite modest cost. It is, in any case, worth while to spend a little more on a really good lens. Second-hand enlargers, provided that they have been well treated by previous owners and are in sound condition, will be more economical again. A trusted dealer will often lend his experience and advice in making a choice and examine the selected equipment for minor faults which may need attention before he parts with it.

Enlarger-lenses, especially on older models, are often not corrected for colour-work. If the making of coloured enlargements is contemplated, a proper colour-corrected lens is indispensable.

ENLARGING AND PRINTING (p. 46)

If tone-rendering of different areas of the subject is not satisfactory in the negative (e.g. a dark foreground remaining evidently underexposed where the main part of the picture has received correct exposure), equal exposure of the whole negative in making the print will only perpetuate the error.

Much can be done to correct such imbalance during exposure of the print. Under-exposed parts (pale on the negative) may be judiciously 'held back' by shading those areas of the image while the darker are being printed up to the proper density. In this way, some little contrast and detail may be brought out, even in the shadows. If fully exposed, these would tend to be lost in the general darkness on the print, even though they were, in fact, recorded on the negative.

Shading during enlarging may be done with the hands alone, but, if the area to be shaded is in the middle of the field, the shadow of the hand cannot be brought over it without that of the arm or sleeve falling also on some part of the margin which needs no shading. A disc of cardboard mounted at the end of a stiff wire will overcome this difficulty. It is kept moving over the required area during some part of the exposure by a hand kept outside the field of view, and so leaves no hard lines.

If it is the centre of the picture which, being relatively dark on the negative, needs to be printed up while only the surroundings are shaded, a sheet of card with a raggedly-torn hole in the middle may be used to shade the margins while passing the required light centrally. The irregular outline of the aperture and constant movement of its area of effect during the exposure prevent any distinct boundary being recorded between the shaded and relatively unshaded areas.

Correct timing of such differential exposures of parts of the negative image during printing requires judgement and practice. This will be achieved at first only by trial and error, but the technique is worth acquiring for the great improvement it may make in obtaining a first-rate enlargement from an imperfect negative.

Contact-prints made on a contact-printing box may be locally shaded during exposure by suitably-shaped pieces of tissue paper with irregularly-torn edges, which are laid on the glass under which the negative is laid and, between it and the light-source. They should not be in direct contact with the negative or the edges of their shadows would print as hard lines. Several layers of tissue may be needed, on occasion, to shade much under-exposed areas of the negative, and these may be made to render detail which would be lost if exposed as fully as the rest of the negative may require. Again, there are no rules! Judgement must be acquired by practice and use.

Different effects may be obtained in enlargements and prints from the selfsame negative by the use of different grades of paper (p. 46). The necessary experience to secure a desired effect should easily be gained by an enthusiastic amateur through trial and error.

DEVELOPMENT

As important a stage as any in the production of a print of satisfactory tonal range is the development. Commercial developers vary greatly and each carries instructions for its proper use in varying circumstances. These must be adhered to strictly, for over- or under-development may modify the inherent degree of contrast given by the grade of paper selected and perhaps entirely spoil the effect aimed at.

As in exposing the print or enlargement by shading some areas while bringing others more quickly forward, the process of development may also be locally intensified or retarded. By immersing a partly-developed print in a stop-bath of water, which rinses the developer-solution off the emulsion, general development may be temporarily suspended. Areas of the print which now require further development may be treated by carefully applying to them more reagent, by means of a finger dipped into the solution. This may bring out local detail which might be lost were the entire print to be evenly developed all over.

An acid, rather than a neutral, fixing-solution is recommended to obtain correctly and permanently fixed prints.

COLOURED ENLARGEMENTS

These can be made from complementary-colour negatives as easily as black-and-white enlargements, after a few experiments and some practice.

Specially-designed enlargers are made for colour-work, but if one of these is not available an existing enlarger can be adapted to serve.

First of all the lens must be colour-corrected. Many enlarger lens are not. A lens similar to that used on the camera is required. Since black-and-white printing papers are insensitive to light at the red end of the spectrum, monochrome enlarging lenses are designed to bring the blue-green and blue rays of white light transmitted by the negative to a sharp focus, disregarding the red and yellow which are ineffective. For full colour-reproduction, however, these too must be capable of critical focusing.

The light-source of the enlarger must be a high-intensity lamp which can be controlled by means of a resistance to secure good colour-balance.

The *tri-colour method* is generally used by amateurs, for the filters are reasonably cheap and adjustment of colour-balance is easily achieved by varying the lengths of the three exposures given to each paper—red, green and blue—in succession. The filters (Tri-colour Gelitron) are generally inserted below the enlarging lens where they can be swung into position easily without any danger of moving the enlarger between exposures, for all three coloured images of the negative must be exactly coincident on the paper to prevent loss of sharpness.

Alternatively the tri-colour filters may be inserted above the negative, but in that case they have to be much larger in area and correspondingly more expensive.

In any case, a heat-absorbing filter must be placed below the lamp, of which

E   51 the heat might otherwise damage the filters. Since the layer of emulsion on the paper designed to record the red image may also be highly sensitive to infrared (heat) radiation, the heat-absorbing filter in front of the lamp is necessary to prevent over-exposure of this layer.

Some colour-papers require a filter (Wratten B.2) to absorb the ultraviolet also, in which case instructions will be included in the packet.

The red safety-filter used between exposures when making black-and-white prints is, of course, ineffective in protecting red-sensitive colour-printing papers. After focusing the light from the enlarger, it must be cut off completely while the paper is positioned for the first exposure, by touch and in darkness, and so, too, while changing the colour-filters between successive exposures. The greatest care must be taken not to shift either the enlarger itself or the paper until all three exposures have been completed.

The *white-light method* calls for a specially-designed enlarger. It does not lend itself to amateur use.

PROCESSING COLOUR ENLARGEMENTS
Papers by various manufacturers vary greatly in sensitivity. It is essential, for satisfactory results, to follow the manufacturers' instructions to the letter.

Chapter six – On the site

On any site which is to be excavated, it is desirable to record the situation before anything is done to it.

In many cases, such as, for instance, a ploughed-out earthwork, there may seem to be very little to see on the ground to show reason why an archaeologist should decide to excavate at all. From the highest obtainable viewpoint, however, at the right time of day and in suitable conditions of weather and light, the presence of slight surface indications may be visible to the eye and, when photographed with the right filter and grade of film, may show features which would escape ordinary observation.

In relatively flat situations the high camera-position may be achieved by the use of a step-ladder, a platform for the tripod, built of boards resting on boxes, by builders' trestles and boards, by a specially-built scaffolding tower, or even by a long ladder propped by a pair of well-splayed scaffold-tubes. A seamanlike job, with adequate lashings and strong stays, is called for here, both for sufficient camera-steadiness and for the mere safety of the photographer's neck!

From such a position, the short focal-length or wide-angle lens will take in a wide enough field to serve the purpose of a general view. If possible, views from several directions taken at different times of day should be tried, to ensure that all points of interest are covered.

Evidently, this will require some time and study of the situation. In any short period of ordinarily changeable weather, the ideal conditions for a particular view are unlikely to present themselves forthwith. If time is limited, the best that can be achieved under the current conditions will have to do, but if there is no undue pressure on the photographer to have done, so that the excavation may proceed, several visits to the site at different times may serve to provide opportunities rather closer to the ideal. Overseas, and especially in Mediterranean lands and the Near East, where meteorological conditions are more reliably predictable, no difficulty should be experienced in quickly achieving presentable photographs of a site before excavation.

In every view, ranging-poles should figure, to give the scales of features at several distances. They must be truly vertical (not too near the edge of the field of a wide-angle lens) and the camera itself should be carefully levelled in two planes at right angles, or with a circular bubble. Ideally, the camera should be tripod-mounted and a cable-release be used to avoid shake, but this will not always be possible from an improvised high vantage-point. With short-focus lenses and reasonably short exposures, the hand-held camera will serve well enough.

Some sites, because of the surrounding topography, may lend themselves to views taken from some little distance and at ground-level. This is where the telephoto lens comes into its own, for its narrow field will cut out neighbouring irrelevancies and its magnification bring the subject close enough to show necessary detail, as if, indeed, the viewer were poised in mid-air at some much closer distance. Seen so, for instance in silhouette against the sky, even some not very distinguished little bumps in the landscape may be made to gain in character and importance. The tripod, the level and the cable-release are all indispensable parts of the equipment for such views.

Where surface indications are but slight and changes in contour not immediately apparent, it will be worth while to keep the camera set up and watch the laying out of the excavation-trenches or squares. A well-dressed line of white pegs, or trench-lines delineated by clean guide-strings crossing features in only low relief will accentuate the changes in slope and show clearly features which, by themselves were not striking even in the best lighting-conditions. Later, the hard lines of well-trimmed trench-edges will serve also to outline the structures which they intersect.

Once digging has begun, the photographer, if not actually engaged in some part of the hand-work, will have to hold himself at the Director's disposal, to record details of interest as they are uncovered and at all the various stages of their further clearance. As each negative is made, the number of the film, its individual frame-number and all technical details of the shot—lens, distance, stop, exposure, filter, etc. must be recorded both in the notebook and, eventually, on the negative bag. Square-number and subject will, of course, be the basic information for identification of the picture. Comments on the viewpoint, direction of view by the compass-bearing, time of day, state of weather and light may not be amiss for future reference.

54

No two excavations are alike. Even in Britain, they may be as diverse as Roman and Medieval remains amid City of London bomb-rubble before rebuilding operations, a high and windy Iron Age hillfort on the Wessex Chalk, some inscrutable small earthwork of unknown date in the depths of a gloomy, dripping pine-wood or the hole-and-corner work in next to total darkness between limestone boulders in a Pleistocene hyaena-den. The archaeological photographer must be, above all things, adaptable!

On a large monument in open country there may be a number of big trenches simultaneously in course of excavation, at widely-separated strategic points. If the foundations of buildings are found, or a complex of post-holes and hearths and pits extending over some area, the first trench may have to be widened into a system of squares with intervening baulks, to pick up the ground-plans of the buried structures. These will almost certainly not coincide neatly with the layout of the excavation, as at first planned.

As the work proceeds, and the nature and plan of the ancient remains emerges, some of the baulks between squares may have to be demolished to lay bare what lies beneath them. Excavation is necessarily progressive removal of layers of deposits of natural or artificial origin, all of which may have something important to tell about the sequence of events at that site, during perhaps successive occupations and eventual decline, or sudden destruction before abandonment and natural burial.

In conjunction with the Director and the actual excavators, it is the photographer's job to record at all stages the progress of the work, so that his pictures may as clearly as possible illustrate the actual appearance of the remains and the deposits covering them as they come to light. Vertical sections will, of course, be drawn to scale by the excavators and the exact positions of finds be plotted into them and into the horizontal plan of the floor of the trench or square in which they lie. The photographs, on the other hand, will provide a completely objective and unbiased view of things, as they actually were. A draughtsman draws what he sees (or *thinks* he sees) and, by selecting what he regards as important, omits what he thinks to be irrelevant. Thus he must fail to include everything, especially things which he was not looking for, and so never noticed. The camera is unselective, recording everything that it can distinguish in the field of view, whether the photographer can understand what he sees before him or not. Naturally, it is as well that he should know what he is photographing, and why, to make sure that all the evidence is presented to the camera in the best possible light, but the apparently irrelevant and the unobserved detail will appear as clearly

55

on the film as the intended point of the picture. In this respect, the photograph is the only *complete* record to survive, of something which will probably no longer exist after the excavation is finished.

Photographing trenches and excavated squares begins with general views, taken from above. If the weather is sunny, some of the sections will be brightly lit while others are in deep, contrasting shadows. For adequate recording of both together, it is best to choose a moment of gentler, diffused light and to consider whether a colour-filter will improve the contrast between layers of different colours but similar tone-values. If other means fail, the flash-gun may be called upon to 'fill in' light which the natural situation does not provide, so as to even out extreme contrasts in a single field of view.

The wide-angle or short-focus lens will be used here, to show the general layout.

Trenches and squares must be tidied up before photographing—all tools and find-trays put out of sight, the vertical walls clean, the floor swept and grass at the edges of the cuts trimmed. This is properly the excavators' job, but the photographer will have to cast a final critical eye over all, to make sure that no irrelevancy intrudes and that all details which must appear in the picture are plainly visible.

There must be at least one scale in every view. If the subject presents some depth, as in looking along the length of a trench, there should be scales in the middle distance and background as well as right before the camera. These may be ranging-poles with clearly painted divisions in feet or metres. For closer views, shorter scales with contrasting black and white subdivisions in inches or centimetres may be laid down or propped up where they are clearly visible, but not obtrusive. Owing to the unavoidable slight distortion at the margins of the image formed by a short-focus lens, vertical scales may have to be adjusted in position and angle so that they *appear* vertical in relation to the sides of the negative, rather than actually being so on the ground. For the same reason, immovable true verticals, such as corners of trenches or angles of baulks, should, as far as possible, appear near the centre of the field rather than at its extreme edges, where they may seem to be leaning into, or out of, the picture, or to be appreciably curved. The notes should state, if it is not already certain from internal evidence, whether the scales are in feet and inches or in metric units. This information is all too often omitted from the captions of published plates!

Human figures may be included in the distance, by way of scale, but they must not merely lean on a shovel and admire the view. Above all, they should not be

56

looking (or grinning!) at the camera, but be *doing something*, if only supporting a ranging-pole or pointing to some important feature of the subject.

The next stage of work will include details of stratification to show the relation of artificial structures to ancient buried land-surfaces and of possible successive occupation-horizons or floors to these and to each other. There may be finds still *in situ*—post-holes, walls, hearths, ovens, pottery, skeletons or cremation-deposits. The latter may be accompanied by grave-goods or offerings. Photographs will be needed to show their exact circumstances before anything is moved—both views to illustrate their general position and close-ups showing detail of structures, equipment, ornaments, etc. This is where ingenuity in cramped corners and the use of all the adaptations of which the camera is capable will have to be mustered to obtain the best results. If a wide-angle lens is used in close-up, can the best light be brought to bear on the subject? If a white or metal reflector is used to improve natural lighting, would not a more distant camera-position, using the telephoto, give a better picture, less subject to any distortion but still giving a large enough image to show all the desired detail? Suppose, even so, that the object extends so much away from the camera that the telephoto lens has not the depth of field to render the whole sharply. Try a very small aperture and a proportionately longer exposure to achieve this. Or is the first really the only possible camera-position? How about another in which the long object can be viewed transversely? Trial and error will often show the simplest way in which to obtain the desired view.

If the point of the picture is to distinguish one layer sharply from another, the slight contrast in tone may be sufficiently brought out by the use of an appropriate filter, if there is a difference in hue which can be exploited. The subject may first be viewed by eye, through various filters in order to weigh up their possible effects, not only on the principal detail, but on the field of view as a whole.

A yellow potsherd, for instance, with a pattern painted in red, all on a background of dark deposit, will best be rendered by the use of a green filter, which will accentuate the contrast between the body of the pot and the painted design. Alternatively, if orthochromatic material (not red-sensitive) is used, even greater contrast may be obtained, but perhaps with some loss of detail in the now darkened red areas of the print.

Any object of a reddish tinge against a dark background may, conversely, be lightened into contrast by using a red filter, and so on.

It is always better, when photographing objects *in situ*, to avoid getting too close in the effort to show maximum detail. Short-focus lenses in close-up inevitably appear to distort to some extent and too near a viewpoint prevents the representation of the true profile of (for example) a more or less globular pot or a human skull completely cleaned for photography, both of which have appreciable depth in relation to their other dimensions. Use a longer-focus lens, or even the telephoto and retire to such a distance that the subject just fills the field, when a close approximation to the true 'elevation'-view will be obtained and distortion be reduced to a minimum.

Once finds have been lifted, they may be removed to the field-studio, for detailed photography in better conditions than can be obtained on the site. If they will stand cleaning (the Director or field-conservator will advise about this if there be any doubt), as much adherent dirt as possible should be gently removed. If not, photography will have to be postponed until proper cleaning and restoration-work have been carried out. Objects of stone or well-fired pottery will not be harmed by a good wash in running water, save in exceptional circumstances.

Small finds and potsherds are best photographed on a shadowless background. This is obtained by laying them out on a horizontal sheet of clean glass or perspex, supported a foot or so (30 cms) above a sheet of white or coloured paper. The camera is set up vertically and if the objects will not lie in the correct attitude for the best lighting of their details, they may be propped up (invisibly!) from behind with pellets or chocks of plasticine. Top lighting should be rather oblique to show the forms of rims, cordons, incisions, raised designs, etc. Back-light must not be too intense, or the result may be a mere silhouette.

Complete pots, standing singly or in groups, are photographed with the camera in the horizontal position. The main light should come from slightly above and to the left, while a reflector on the right, also directed downwards from slightly above the subject, may be used to soften shadows and show some detail on the darker side. This will give depth and modelling and show up the rims to advantage. A background of paper or cloth, at some distance behind the subject, and so out of focus, will eliminate their shadows and any irrelevancies beyond. If cloth is used, it may be hung from a high rail, placed well back and out of the field of view, and be brought forward under the subject and draped over another rail below it.

If pots are grouped, they should not stand so close together that the reflected side-light cannot 'kill' any shadows between them. The camera view-point should be slightly above the rims, so that the open mouths of the pots can be seen. Every picture must include a scale and different groups should be identified by a neatly written or printed label seen at the extreme edge of the field and corresponding with their numbers in the register of finds.

58

TOMBS, TUNNELS, CAVES

The wide-angle lens is almost essential in such usually cramped quarters, as is flash for the lighting. Focusing of the subject, if darkness is total, will be carried out by the light of an electric torch, lamp or even candle, placed at an appropriate distance in the middle of the field of view. Several flashes may be required, from different points. If any of these positions is in front of the camera, the actual flash (and the operator, if it is not remotely controlled!) must be carefully shielded from the lens, in a recess or round a corner. The combined effect of multiple flashes requires careful preliminary planning, using several lamps simultaneously lighting the subject from the intended flash-sites. The camera shutter may be left open, at 'time', between flashes. This is essential if the 35 mm miniature is in use, for, here, shutter cocking is coupled with the film wind-on mechanism, specially to *prevent* unintentional double exposures. Once tripped, the shutter cannot be re-cocked to expose the same frame. With the shutter open, a solitary photographer will have to move in total darkness from one flash-site to the next. In such a case special care must be taken not to trip over the tripod, an accident which can occur only too easily! It is obviously better to have one or more assistants to set off the flashes (all keeping well out of sight meanwhile): then, nobody need move in darkness and all will be well.

BANKS AND DITCHES, RAMPARTS

The camera-viewpoint and different conditions of light need careful consideration when we are dealing with earthworks. Only by watching the subject through the changing lights of the day can one determine the best moment to expose, which will ensure capturing the effect desired.

The camera-position should not be too high, in order that the outline of the bank may stand out clearly against the distant background and the sky. Rather oblique, even lighting will detach the structures from their background and give a certain depth to the picture. Any colour-contrast may be emphasised by the choice of an appropriate filter. A diffused light, as with sun veiled by thin clouds, will bring out details in a ditch, which might be too deeply shadowed in full sunlight to show anything at all.

Tall grass moving in the wind may cast deceptive, blurred shadows and falsely suggest changes in relief where there is none on the ground. So, too, with tree-shadows. If unavoidable by the choice of a more suitable time of day, or conditions of more diffused light, their movement may be minimized by the choice of a fast shutter-speed, the corresponding larger aperture required being read off the light-meter.

In the presence of haze, or even with mist lying in ditches and depressions, wait, if possible, for better conditions. If there can be no choice of time, a red filter with panchromatic film will eliminate most of the haze, but will also seriously affect the tone-rendering of greens, with possible consequential loss. Dark green turf will be reproduced as a very pale tone in the print and perhaps lose its natural contrast with areas of bare chalk (for instance), to the detriment of the picture as a whole. Infrared, however advisable to cut out mistiness, will make this tone-distortion even more prominent. It may well be acceptable in the circumstances, but one must always bear in mind the possible secondary effects on the colours in the visible waveband of using extreme filters.

For general views of earthworks and defences, use the normal-focus lens. A trench section taking in both ditch and bank will call for the wide-angle, positioned at a fairly high viewpoint. Any details to be photographed standing in the trench itself, where there is no possibility of retiring to a normal working distance, will also require the wide-angle lens. Watch for undue distortion of straight lines and verticals near the edges of the field. Again, these may have to be accepted in the interests of recording whatever it is, where it is, from the only possible photographic viewpoint.

Pits. Crop-marks in aerial photographs are often the first indications of the presence on a site of artificially-dug pits. If any signs are visible at ground-level, they should be recorded in a general view, taken from the highest point available, before excavation starts. Since, on arable land, the crop will generally first have been reaped or lifted, it is likely that no visible evidence will remain, but, in pasture, slight differences in depth of colour of the grass may be discernible. In that case, a suitable filter will serve to emphasise these on panchromatic film.

On lifting the turf or clearing the plough-soil, the generally moister, dark, humic pit-fillings should appear in some contrast with the general subsoil colour, on a well-scraped and brushed surface. Another view, to show the distribution of the pits, should be taken at this point. Since the trowelled surface will be flat, colour or tone only, not relief, will distinguish the pits from their surroundings. It may be possible to intensify the contrast by discreet water-spraying after cleaning. If not, selection of the proper colour-filter may serve to exploit a difference in hue between filling and subsoil.

It is usual to take out only half the pit-filling, across a diameter, at first, to show any stratification and so elucidate the processes by which the filling has been formed. This possibly presents the photographer with a difficult subject, especially in the case of a deep and narrow-mouthed pit. Not only will adequate lighting be a problem, but the full field in close-up of the wide-angle lens will be needed to encompass the whole depth of the feature in a single shot. The required depth of field demands the smallest practicable aperture and so, possibly, a long exposure. A yellow-green general-contrast filter will distinguish coloured layers. The line of sight will necessarily be very oblique to the face of the subject, unless some area of subsoil can be cleared in front of the pit and the whole structure be exposed in half-section. Unless this is so, the bottom of the hole will inevitably be dark in comparison with the upper part. If full sun gives adequate illumination here, a flash from the camera-position may be needed to 'fill in' the shaded part below.

Should the ground be unduly wet, or there even be a pool of water lying in the bottom of the pit, it may be possible to obtain a good view only by breaking this surface which may reflect the sky, or even an image of the camera and operator. A pebble or small clod of earth may be dropped into the pool at the moment of exposure. It is well to experiment first to find out the best size of missile which will just achieve this object without undue disturbance or splash!

Should there be any find—for instance, a cremation-urn—at the bottom of a pit, it may be seen *in situ* from a high position using the telephoto lens. A flash from the camera-position may be necessary to light the subject sufficiently. Provided that the flash were well shielded from the lens, it could be brought right up to the lip of the pit, in front, if the equipment could be excluded from the field of view. This should often not be difficult, considering the narrow field of the telephoto.

Using a little judgement and ingenuity in the choice of lenses, filters, lighting, apertures and exposure-times should make it possible to obtain an usable picture of almost any subject. Archaeological materials stand obligingly still, giving plenty of time for forethought, trial and error in positioning and so on. Undue haste is the enemy of good photography at any time—and here, above all, it is unnecessary!

Once lifted and somewhat cleaned (a job for the conservator, this!) more detailed records can be made of the find in the field-studio (p. 83).

ULTRAVIOLET PHOTOGRAPHY IN THE FIELD

Suitable portable field-equipment, consisting of one or more battery-powered U.V. lamps with spare batteries, is not yet on the market. The prototype was specially designed for the London University Institute of Archaeology, from which information may be obtained as to the supplier.

Where visible fluorescence of some archaeological object is to be recorded, a 2B U.V. absorption filter is required before the camera-lens to cut out ultraviolet radiation reflected from the subject.

For the plate-camera, Ilford Zenith plates are recommended. They are fast and give excellent results. For the 35 mm miniature format, Kodak Recording film, with a speed of 1,000 Weston is most satisfactory.

Since fluorescence under U.V. radiation is faint at the best of times, total darkness is required during the necessarily fairly long exposure. This can be achieved in the field, in daylight, only by a perfectly light-tight tent, large enough to contain the subject, the lighting equipment, the camera and its tripod and even the person of the photographer himself.

The lamps are positioned near the ground, but well out of the field of view and at different distances. Since their U.V. output is fixed, the only way of varying the intensity of illumination of the object is by changing the distance between the lamps and it.

The exposure required will depend on these distances (applying the Inverse Square Law—twice the distance: four times the exposure) and on the short or long view taken by the camera—the closer the view, the longer the exposure. Trial and error will be needed for first attempts and all results, however unsatisfactory, should be scrupulously recorded in the notebook, for future reference. Only in this way can errors be corrected in future.

Any substance which will fluoresce under U.V. lends itself to photographic accentuation by this method. Among the more common are some minerals occurring in hard rocks and sediments, including fossil bones embedded in cave-deposits and human or animal skeletons found on archaeological sites. Some organic substances are also fluorescent. In such cases, and especially when ordinary lighting, even with the aid of colour-filters, is unable to distinguish between an object and the matrix in which it is embedded, fluorescence under U.V. radiation may solve the photographic problem outright.

Indoors or in the museum, U.V. may facilitate the recording of otherwise invisible traces of fluorescent materials in pictures, wall-paintings, manuscripts or archaeological objects. In the latter case, glues and invisibly-mended portions will often show up original imperfections, perhaps fraudulently made good by an unscrupulous restorer or dealer, in order to obtain a better price. There are, of course, entire forgeries which may sometimes be detected by a photograph under U.V.

Chapter seven – Field details

Several photographs should be taken of an entire skeleton or group of bones, during the process of their exposure, clearing and cleaning for the final picture. This will ensure the existence of some record in case of any accidental disturbance or breakage during that often delicate operation. If burials have suffered any ancient disturbance, it will be necessary to show its nature and extent, and, if any bones have to be lifted in order to expose others beneath them, a whole series of photographs will be necessary. This is just like the technique of serial-sectioning for a three-dimensional histological study, to expose a number of surfaces in succession and record the disposition of the structures in depth, as well as on any one surface. This was, for instance, carried out at the pre-pottery Neolithic cemetery at Jericho, where several skulls had been robbed out from a group of burials after only a short interval, so that the remains of numbers of individual skeletons were inextricably mixed.

Correctly prepared for final recording, the parts of a skeleton should appear in bold relief, supported from beneath by props of the surrounding matrix left in position for that purpose, so that nothing has been disturbed or moved and the exposed surfaces have been cleaned as well as possible. If the bones do not show enough tone-contrast with the matrix, an appropriate filter may be used to heighten it, but if they are well preserved and skilfully prepared, oblique lighting devised by means of reflectors, using daylight, or by flash, if natural light does not lend itself, will cast shadows not too intense, giving the necessary contrast and relief. In open situations, direct sunlight, if not too intense, will serve, but if the find is at the bottom of a deep, narrow trench, grave or pit, some such artificial aids to lighting may be required. Direct sun is, on the whole, to be avoided, for if the highlights are correctly exposed, there will necessarily be some loss of detail in the shadows. Further, direct sun is bad for bones still *in situ*, with one side still embedded in moist earth while the exposed cleaned surface is drying rapidly. This may well lead to uneven shrinkage and cracking.

Where the bones are poorly preserved, decalcified, in crumbs or even represented only by a darker 'ghost' of the skeleton on clean subsoil, photography under U.V. radiation may show more detail than a picture in ordinary light. Owing to the long exposure necessary to record faint fluorescence, all daylight must be excluded and this is best done in the field by erecting a small tent of black, light-proof material over the area selected. A camera of small (Rolleiflex) or miniature (35 mm) format is desirable, to concentrate all available light into a small image and so reduce the inevitably long exposure.

A high-speed (1000 Weston) film is used, with an ultraviolet (2B) absorbing filter over the lens, to eliminate reflected U.V. and pass only the fluorescent rays in the visible spectrum. The U.V. source may be a battery-powered lamp, of which the bulk and weight is nowadays much less than it was, with increased portability.

The bones, or their residues, mineral and organic, fluoresce and may yield an image on the film much better defined than any visible to the eye under ordinary illumination. A fine-grain developer is desirable, used for twice the recommended development-time at a temperature of about 68°F, no matter what type of film is used.

Cremated bones (calcined—all organic matter destroyed) do not fluoresce with U.V. radiation. If even colour-filters fail to give satisfactory contrast between them and their background in ordinary light, it is worth trying infrared illumination. Focusing is done through a deep red filter (the visible band nearest in wavelength to I.R.). For the exposure it is best replaced by an infrared filter (Kodak 88A) and the negative material must be Kodak I.R. extra-rapid plate or film. Accurate fine-grain development will be necessary.

MOSAICS AND TESSELLATED PAVEMENTS

The first step is to photograph the entire area, showing the relation of the floor to walls, doorways, etc. Suitable scales, and perhaps an arrow showing the north-point, should be included. The subject will require a high viewpoint for the camera and the wide-angle lens. Even, overall illumination must be obtained, so that the best time of day and quality of the light must be taken into consideration to avoid too-deep shadows from surrounding walls, with consequent loss of detail in relatively under-lighted corners.

In photographing a coloured pavement in monochrome, it is not the colours themselves that matter, but their tone-values. A filter will be chosen, after first

64

inspection by eye trying the effects of several, preferably clearly to distinguish all colours by their tones but, for instance, to bring out at least a palish yellow in contrast to the adjacent white tesserae of the background, in a case where (say) red, blue and black may be expected to take care of themselves. On the whole, a pale green filter is likely to render tones much as the eye sees them, on panchromatic material. In the particular case above, perhaps one somewhat yellow-green, rather than blue-green, would be most effective.

Secondly, a compound picture may be required, consisting of a number of conjoined vertical views, taken from close enough to each section to show individual tesserae and any minor irregularities (due, perhaps, to repairs carried out in ancient times), the separate frames later to be fitted together to represent the entire pavement in close-up.

The wide-angle lens, with its marginal distortions, will not do here, for fitting and matching the edges of the eventual prints will be most difficult. The short- or normal-focus lens should be used, allowing plenty (up to 30% on each side) of overlap of field between adjacent exposures.

The trick, in piecing together overlapping prints is to trim off the margins, match up (as well as possible) the edge of one with the middle part of the next and, clipping the two together in this position, to cut, with scissors or guillotine, along a line half way across the overlap. This exactly distributes the refractive errors of the lens between the two prints and makes the cut edges match very closely. Two adjacent images made by any lens will never match perfectly when placed edge-to-middle.

The pavement should be thoroughly swept and cleaned just before photographing. Damping the surface with water generally brings up the colours, but any differences in dampness, or uneven drying between exposures will make it hard to match up the prints. Adding glycerine to the water retards evaporation and makes the effect more durable, but, even so, a perfectly uniform degree of moisture has to be achieved if the adjacent prints are not to show irremediable differences in tone. If a good picture is at all possible otherwise, damping should be avoided.

The camera should be in a position of exactly equal height for each exposure, checked each time by measurement to avoid even slight differences in magnification. The back of the camera must be levelled in two directions at right-angles to ensure verticality. There must be a scale in the field of each negative, near the edge to be trimmed off, to ensure uniform dimensions in the eventual prints.

Panchromatic film without a filter will give adequate colour contrast and a fairly soft negative, of which the contrast will be built up to the required degree in printing. Filters are only needed to emphasise contrast between particular features of coloured subjects like pavements or wall-paintings.

GRAVES

The treatment of graves will be very similar to that described for pits—a generally high viewpoint for the camera, several photographs during clearing and the same kinds of devices to overcome possibly awkward camera-angles and uneven lighting. As before, diffused daylight, rather than direct sun, will best serve our purpose.

In excavating graves, it is always important, if possible, to determine the level of the ancient surface from which they were dug, in order to assign reliable dates to burials which may be unaccompanied by grave-goods or internal dating-evidence, such as coins. From the photographer's point of view, this will come down to recording convincingly any such stratigraphical evidence—the discordance, for instance, between the grave-fill and any overlying intact and datable stratum, than which the grave must be earlier.

In many instances the whole plan of the burial will not lie clearly in the trench or square which first exposed it, so that the required stratigraphical evidence for its date should be visible in the section of the trench-wall, where the unexplored part of the grave runs under it, or the baulk between adjacent squares of which it is part. The recording of this will, perhaps, be less tricky than that of finds in a narrow, deep pit, but the same kinds of problems are likely to present themselves— uneven lighting, restricted choice of camera-angles and working distances, lack of tone-contrast between different strata exposed in the section and the physical difficulties of preparing and photographing a skeleton in a confined space.

COFFINS

The wood of a coffin may have perished almost completely, leaving only a stain, which, in dark-coloured earth, may be scarcely distinguishable by eye. In pale-coloured sand or chalk, on the other hand, the traces of the coffin may be clearly visible. The yellow-green filter with panchromatic film will adequately render any distinction in tone which is appreciable to the eye. If there are noticeable differences in hue, the appropriate colour-filter will accentuate the naked-eye contrast.

For close-up recording of objects associated with a burial (for example, beads of a necklace or a bronze shoulder-brooch in position), the field-camera with double extension or extension-rings or bellows on a miniature type, both used with the normal lens, will enable the close approach needed to illustrate the detail *in*

66

situ. Depth of field will be small, so a position must be chosen from which as much of the subject as possible lies in, or near to the picture-plane. The supplementary lens (p. 16), fitted like a filter in front of the normal lens, is an inexpensive and too often despised aid to close-ups, if the more modern and flexible equipment referred to is not available.

POST-HOLES

These, like pits and graves, will appear in plan with some contrast of colour or consistency (e.g. a loamy filling in chalk) on a well-scraped and brushed occupation-surface. In most cases there is likely to be little trace of the original post, but occasionally remains of decayed wood or charcoal may be found still in position. To record these, it is generally best to have the hole and its immediate surroundings cleared, to present a clean, vertical section, when the size and shape of the former post can be seen and the positions of any chock-stones used to wedge it in firmly.

Any complex of post-holes showing the layout of a structure, such as a hut or granary, should first be recorded together in plan after careful cleaning. For vertical photographs of any considerable area a high camera-point is required, which is not often available, but may sometimes be improvised (p. 53). In general, a relatively high oblique view will serve, including scales at suitable distances. Treatment will call for diffused oblique daylight (early or late in the day), a lens of focal length adapted to the lateral extent and depth of the subject, a small aperture if the depth is appreciable and a chosen colour-filter to obtain the desired contrast.

This general view will be followed by close-ups of individual post-holes to show features of interest—wood-remains, chock-stones, etc. Colours concerned are likely to be yellows and browns, more or less distinguished by greyish or reddish tinges. Yellow or red filters may pick these out from the background.

Even the infrared filter and negative material may make it possible, in direct sun, for the camera to distinguish detail invisible to the eye. It is at least worth trying more often than is generally done, for the results are fairly unpredictable.

PHOTOPLANNING

This is, perhaps, a better term for the taking of vertical photographs on archaeological sites than 'Photogrammetry'. The latter is a far more elaborate, exact and expensively-equipped branch of photographic surveying for which neither the techniques nor the apparatus fall within the compass of most excavators and photographers.

The more modest object of photoplanning is to produce exactly-scaled vertical views of a site or (more often) parts of a site, if the necessarily high viewpoint cannot be made high enough to take the whole excavation into the field of view of a single exposure. If verticals of adjacent areas are taken separately at exactly the same scale, with sufficient overlaps, as in aerial mapping, the resultant prints may be subsequently joined together into a mosaic to present an accurate vertical plan of the excavation in its entirety.

A site on which considerable areas are opened up will, in any case, have been carefully laid out in measured trenches or squares before beginning work and the object of the photoplan, like that of any archaeological photograph, is to present to scale a quite objective view of the major structures and details to be seen, without the selectivity as to what is to be shown inseparable from the best and most detailed hand-drawn plan. Owing to the camera's shortcomings, however, in the matter of lens-aberrations, distortion of perspective, un-flatness of field and so on, unless the photographs are taken with great care to minimise these or with specially engineered (and, accordingly, expensive) highly corrected equipment, the prints will not compare for over-all dimensional accuracy with a drawn scale-plan based on measurements taken direct on the ground.

The essentials for photoplanning are a stable high-viewpoint mount for the camera, means of levelling the latter exactly, so that the optical axis is always truly vertical, a lens with minimum aberrations and flat field and accurately-positioned and surveyed fixed points on the ground in the field of view.

HIGH POINT CAMERA-MOUNT, LEVELLING, ETC.

Designed for military, civil-engineering or police photogrammetry, there is commercially available a free-standing pneumatically-operated tubular telescopic mast* weighing 52 lb, giving a maximum extension of 40 ft for a camera-load of up to 10 lb. This costs £200, which is more than most individual excavations could afford.

An army-surplus surveying tripod, with a telescopic extension to a height of 11 ft would be much less expensive at second-hand prices. A further extension might be designed for this to increase the working-height, but both would have to be lowered between exposures to wind on the film and reset the shutter. In any case a firm, well-stayed horizontal arm to carry the camera would be needed, so that its field of view was clear of the tripod legs and other supports.

A remotely-controlled or automatic levelling system for the camera would be necessary. With the regular photogrammetric mast referred to above, the camera

* Made by Messrs. A. N. Clark (Engineering) Ltd., Binstead, Isle of Wight.

is carried in a special cradle originally designed by the Road Research Laboratory for their own purposes. The shutter is electrically operated and the current has to pass through three mercury micro-switches which close the circuit simultaneously only when the lens-axis is perfectly vertical. Something like this, using a well-damped but responsive gimbal-suspension and mercury-switches should not be beyond the wit of an amateur engineer to construct, for far less than a commercial price.

A plumb line running over a pulley at some fixed position and distance from the lens-axis is required to ensure that the vertical lens is centred on the area to be photographed. This is lowered to coincide with a point on the ground, similarly offset to correct parallax, and is then hauled up again out of the field of view when the camera is correctly positioned for an exposure. If no electrical release can be devised a sufficient length of cable release will have to be used.

Lens. With a 35 mm miniature camera the normal lens of 50 mm focal length will be best for this work. A wide-angle lens would cover a given area with fewer exposures (and of course give a smaller image) but the errors of even an ordinarily good wide-angle towards the edges of its field are unacceptable when it comes to fitting together the mosaic of prints into an accurate plan.

Both kites and gas-balloons have been used in the past for taking high verticals. The impossibility of positioning them, steadying and controlling their movements with sufficient accuracy rules them out for photoplanning purposes. They would serve well enough for oblique aerial snapshots.

Chapter eight – Buildings and interiors

ARCHITECTURE

Although more bulky and heavy than others, the field-camera with its corrective movements (p. 1) is the ideal instrument for photographing architectural subjects.

According to the area to be covered by the picture, lenses of different focal-lengths will be used—normal lens for middle distance, short focal-length lens for wider coverage, the wide-angle for unavoidably close-up positions where there is no space for manoeuvre. The telephoto may be used for recording detail inaccessible from closer-range—distant buildings or inscriptions high up on façades of those near by.

The rising front prevents exaggerated perspective (converging perpendiculars), unavoidable if the whole camera is tilted to take in a high building. If the front has, in any case, to be tilted to cover the subject, parallelism of the image may be restored by using the tilting back. Perspective is thus improved and inclusion of over much foreground avoided.

The miniature camera, on the other hand, not provided with these movements, will inevitably give false perspective with such subjects. The use of the wide-angle lens will reduce the degree of tilt and so minimise the effect.

The hand- and stand-camera falls between these two extremes. It will at least have a rising front, even if this and the back are not also tiltable. With the adjustable lens-panel the full range of lenses of different focal lengths is available.

The pictorial effect of buildings may be modifiable by the use of panchromatic film and appropriate filters. If one of white or dull yellow stone is the subject, a yellow or red filter will lighten the tone of the building in contrast with a dramatically darkened blue sky or misty distant background. The same filters will bring out the contrast also of dull red brickwork with a darker background, thereby intensifying the lighting of the interesting subject and making it stand out in the picture.

70

Focusing of architectural subjects should always be carried out at full aperture, and this can afterwards be stopped down before exposing to give the maximum overall sharpness of image.

MUSEUMS, CASTLES, CHURCHES, INTERIORS, ARCHITECTURE AND OBJECTS

When setting out, permission to photograph should if possible have been pre-arranged. There may exist restrictions as to the use (for instance) of flash-equipment, tripods, and the larger types of camera, and in applying it will save time if the equipment proposed is specified, and the eventual purpose of the photographs, for such restrictions normally apply only to those intended for commercial or professional use. Photography for research or recording purposes only will normally be unrestricted if due permission is obtained.

Equipment. The miniature camera is usually preferred if many pictures are to be taken. For interior architecture and detail work, nevertheless, the field- or stand-cameras, with their corrections for perspective and larger format for recording detail, remain extremely valuable. A check-list would include lenses of all available focal lengths, lens-hood, several filters, spirit-level, focusing magnifier, scales, light-meter and the flash-outfit. A dark loading-bag is invaluable for correcting any wind-on trouble in roll-film cameras, loading slides, developing in an emergency, or loading film-tanks. A roll of paper to be used for backgrounds and a large light-weight black cloth are useful additions. The latter is valuable for shading out distracting reflections in the glazing of showcases or pictures and serves as wrapping for packed equipment when not in use. A polarising filter is also useful for cutting out unwanted reflections and too-intense highlights from the polished surfaces of objects. The polariser, since it selects only part of the available light for admission to the lens, will demand a suitable increase in exposure.

INTERIORS

Even in fairly well-lit interiors it is generally necessary to use time-exposures, for some areas may remain in shadow. Heavy shadow may be relieved by a well-placed flash trained on the underlit area of a subject. Even without the flash, an exposure intermediate between the extremes of light and dark parts of the field of view, as measured with the light-meter, will bring up sufficient detail in the shaded parts.

When using the field-camera, allowance must be made for the spreading of the available light over the area of the large negative by giving a somewhat longer exposure than that specified by the meter. Such is the latitude of modern black and white negative material that over-exposure even by a factor of three will still yield an acceptable negative. Meter-readings are only a guide, to be modified from one's experience according to any special circumstances. For example, when using the miniature camera in poor light or in a close-up view two or three times the meter reading would not, perhaps, be too much. Judgment may be aided by comparing meter-readings at different distances from the subject, noting the effect of diminishing illumination with closer approach to it.

For interior detail, such as a carved capital on a tall column, the telephoto lens will prove its worth. In a tight corner the wide-angle lens may provide the only answer to the problem. Pictures taken with both of them will be improved by the use of a small aperture and a longer exposure time. For this purpose the tripod will be essential to avoid camera-shake. Even at higher speeds, say up to 100th sec, the use of a tripod will ensure maximum definition.

When light is adequate, as for instance with a high ceiling or where stonework or interior decorations are light in colour, it is preferable to use a slow film, such as ASA 50. The fine grain will render the subject in full detail while, using a faster film, even with the correspondingly small aperture, the coarser grain of the negative may result in an overall greyness and loss of contrast.

WINDOW DETAILS

Direct strong light falling on a window, even one of stained glass, should be avoided if possible. Early morning or evening light is gentler and more oblique. If it is unavoidable to photograph a window through which light is entering directly towards the camera, a polarizing filter may cut down glare. Further, over-exposing by up to three times the meter-reading and under-developing will result in a softer negative and the flatness of this may be improved during printing by accentuating the highlights and holding back the shadows.

OBJECTS

These can frequently not be moved to improve their photographic potential. In a case where one side is in deep shadow a white reflector outside the field of view may be used to throw enough light on to that side to show some detail. Similarly, if artificial lighting is used to even up the illumination, it should fall predominantly on the darker side.

For such highly reflective objects as glazed pots, glass or silverware the too intense highlights may be softened, without detracting from their proper polished

72

appearance, by using a diffuser before the light source—muslin, ground glass, tissue-paper.

Objects photographed from too short a distance may suffer some distortion of outline or partial loss of sharpness, especially when their depth is a considerable fraction of the viewing distance. If space is not restricted, retiring to a more distant viewpoint and using the long-focus, or even the telephoto, lens will give a truer profile view and improvement in overall definition, especially if a small aperture is used.

Objects in *show-cases* which may not be opened for photography present special problems, notably that of mirroring the camera itself and its operator if the lens axis is normal to the glass. If possible the view may be taken a little obliquely to the reflecting surface and any other reflections from beyond be masked out by a flat black cloth strategically draped. If the camera *must* be used normally to the glass, the black cloth should have a hole just large enough to pass the lens, masking all the rest. Preferably the case should be lighted from inside only and all the surroundings be dark, when external reflections will be unimportant. A polarizing filter adjusted by rotation may help to minimise unwanted reflections but is unlikely to cut them all out completely.

Paintings under glass or with a glossy varnish may similarly give reflections of well-lighted objects in front of them. The best way of avoiding this is (if possible) to darken the room or gallery by lowering blinds or drawing curtains of windows opposite to the subject and, if necessary, to light it artificially, obliquely from one or both sides of the camera. Failing this, the viewpoint will have to be moved to avoid the worst reflections even if the receding parallels of the frame then converge perceptibly. With the field camera the perspective can be corrected, but not with the miniature, in which case the best compromise between reflections and oblique perspective will have to be accepted. In many cases unavoidable reflections may not be too prominent on the eventual print.

MOVING-LIGHT METHOD FOR LIGHTING ARTIFICIAL-LIGHT
INTERIORS OR STUDIO SUBJECTS

In some cases of interior photography, where the existing fixed lighting is uneven or inadequate, and even in the studio in the case of a difficult subject with high tone-contrast or awkward relief, a light-source moved about by hand during a time exposure may enable detail to be brought out in shaded areas and extreme tone-contrasts to be softened.

The successful use of this device is, obviously, very much a matter of experience and judgement. Every subject is an individual and no general instructions will serve to ensure first-time success in a particular case. The variable factors involved are:

(1) Intensity of light given by the moving source;

(2) Distance of the source from the parts of the object to be lighted (the inverse-square law will come in here—halve the distance: multiply $\times 4$ the light intensity received by the object);

(3) Relative time (fraction of the total exposure) during which the light from the moving source is allowed to fall on each part of the object.

The general effect of a moving lamp is to distribute light more evenly, i.e. to avoid concentrated reflections from a highly polished surface, fill in deep shadows where fixed lighting might not penetrate and soften shadows cast by the objects on the background, supporting surface or other nearby objects.

Interiors of large buildings or rooms in which no rearrangement of furniture or objets d'art is permissible are obvious candidates for this treatment. The moving single lamp of power appropriate to the depth and width of the camera's field of view, will throw up detail hitherto shadowed and make a picture out of a view which could not otherwise be illuminated sufficiently with anything less than a battery of studio floods and spotlights.

If using a stand-camera of larger format, in which, because of the area of plate to be covered and a nevertheless small stop used to gain maximum depth of focus, a fairly long time-exposure will be needed. There will then be plenty of time to arrange a quite complicated series of movements of the lamp to build up a satisfactory over-all effect.

Though some trial-and-error will be needed to gain the experience required to have confidence every time in one's own judgement, sensible advance planning of a moving-light exposure will avoid the worst mistakes, inevitable if going by pure guesswork.

Once it has been calculated about what length of exposure would be needed for suitable lighting of the subject by a number of stationary lamps used all together, their positions and directions may successively be adopted by the single light to build up the same total exposure over an extended time.

In the studio, groups of small objects, bones or coins for half-tone plates may usefully be illuminated in this way. With the camera in the vertical position over the group, the lamp will light it generally from the top of the picture. In the case of one including both dark and light-coloured objects such as bronze coins with white plaster casts for comparison the dark will, if possible, be arranged at the top nearest to the lamp. During the exposure the lamp will be moved a little from side to side, now close to the plane of the group to give very oblique lighting, now higher to the front to wash out long shadows caused by the former; concentrating for longer on the darker objects, only briefly on the light. This will give a more evenly-lit negative, showing all the necessary detail but without totally eliminating differences in tone between different materials.

Chapter nine – Studio work

PHOTOGRAPHY IN THE STUDIO

In a well-designed studio for archaeological photography we have aimed at conditions as nearly perfect for producing good work as the space and equipment at our disposal permit and our own ingenuity can devise. Every different kind of lighting, a varied choice of backgrounds and flexible but firm camera mounts for producing a fine negative have been provided. The facilities of the processing and enlargement sections should enable the best possible print to be made from that negative, which can finally be neatly and tastefully mounted for display if so required.

Studio work is aimed at producing photographs of archaeological finds, not only for display or for publication (though this is obviously an important primary function), but for research to record the results of (say) conservation treatment of an object through all its stages, so that ancient methods and techniques used in its manufacture can be studied as well as the processes of decay or corrosion to which it has since been subject. Good photographs will provide permanent records of an object's condition before, during and after conservation, so that the value of the treatment given can be assessed and the gradual development of significant details during transitional stages of cleaning and preservation be observed. To this end we have installed equipment for ultra-violet and infrared illumination of the subject, for close-up ('macro') views of fine detail and study of its structure at even higher magnifications, if necessary, by means of photomicrography, in full colour when required.

We now turn to the various main classes of archaeological subjects, to discuss how they should be treated in greater detail.

POTTERY

Entire pots should be arranged well in front of a contrasting background so as to give some depth to the picture and be lighted both from above and from the sides

76

to render their own roundness accurately. Every group should include a scale, and this must be in proportion to the dimensions of the whole composition and of the individual vessels. The scale must cast no interfering shadow in the chosen conditions of lighting. This is best avoided by positioning the scale horizontally near the plane of the objects, ensuring that the lettering distinguishing inch- from centimetre-graduations is included, even should it be partly cut off at the margin of the picture by eventual trimming of the print.

Rims of pots are important. The camera viewpoint should be slightly above the mouths of the pots and these should appear sharp all round even when the openings are relatively wide (as, for instance, in a large dish or a shallow basin). This may be ensured by the use of a small aperture, giving sufficient depth of field, or by increasing the distance of the camera, fitted with a long-focus, or even a telephoto, lens. In any case the camera should not be so close to the subject that perceptible distortion in depth is caused—the ideal view of it should present the objects as nearly as possible in true profile. Too close a viewpoint is a common fault in such photographs.

Pots with handles should be so positioned that at least one of the handles is seen in true profile, well set off by its background.

Top lighting from in front of the subject may cast an unwanted shadow on the background in the case of a broad-based flat-bottomed pot. This may be avoided or at least improved by bringing the pot slightly forward or by making the background material recede out of focus at a rather sharper angle.

Decorations in relief on pots may be accentuated by the use of more oblique lighting.

If decoration in flat colours does not stand out clearly, suitable colour-filters will accentuate the tone-contrast between the paint and the ground-colour of the pot. Consideration will have to be given, here, not only to the colours of the pot but to that of the lighting, and to the type of film being used. Even photofloods give a much lower-colour-temperature (yellower) light than daylight and this may materially affect colour rendering and tonal contrast.

Developer-formula and developing-time may be adjusted in special cases to achieve desired contrasts in the negative.

Some British Iron Age coarse pottery is very undistinguished in appearance but with skilled arrangement and lighting may nevertheless be enhanced in character as a group. Finely scratched or shallowly-incised decoration may be brought out by careful lighting and even differences in fine texture of undecorated areas be accentuated to give interest.

Glazed pottery presents quite different problems. Ground-glass or fibreglass diffusers on the lamps will soften too glaring highlights and so enable details of decoration even in weak tone-contrast to be shown. Polarizing filters would serve the same purpose, but may also introduce unnatural-looking effects in lighting.

Small pots should, if possible, be photographed separately from the larger. Their treatment will, in principle, be similar to that devised for bigger vessels, but with camera-position, lens, and lighting adjusted to make the most of their finer detail. Avoidance of irrelevant shadows is just as important as before and will be achieved by adjustment of lighting, background and auxiliary reflectors.

SHERDS OF POTTERY

Whole pots are the exception rather than the rule in most excavations. Most publications will require photographs of groups of representative sherds.

Groups of sherds are laid out neatly, rims (if any, or at least upper parts) to the top of the picture, the outer edges of each group conforming to the straight lines of a notional rectangular frame centred on the actual rectangle of the negative. The arrangement is made, for a vertical camera position, on a horizontal sheet of glass or perspex raised about 10″ (25 cms) above a suitable background-sheet of paper curving down from its upper edge (as seen by the camera) to cover the whole background. Sherds should be (invisibly!) propped if necessary in the most advantageous position by strategically-placed blobs of plasticine.

Lighting may be either by daylight or the studio lamps and should fall obliquely from the 'north-west', using a narrow vertical reflector-sheet, out of sight at the foot of the group, to fill in any unduly heavy shadows cast by the rims. Every group must have a clearly legible scale of suitable dimensions, neatly placed and lying strictly parallel with the lower edge of the group. If, owing to relatively high curvature of larger sherds, the group has appreciable 'depth', a small enough lens-aperture must be chosen to ensure that both nearest and furthest parts are acceptably sharp in focus and the exposure time be increased accordingly.

Consideration should next be given to the type of negative emulsion to be used and whether any colour-filter is necessary to accentuate painted decoration. If so, viewing the group by eye through appropriate filters will show what their effects will be on an eventual print. Infrared-sensitive film will emphasise black or dark-coloured patterns which are worn or of low contrast in ordinary light. If the paint has a metallic lustre, fluorescence arising from ultraviolet illumination will accentuate its brilliance.

HAND-AXES OR OTHER FLAKED-FLINT IMPLEMENTS

These may be treated in much the same way as potsherds—grouped neatly with a scale, points or working edges to the top of the picture and, on the whole, lit at a fairly low angle from the top left-hand corner. Plasticine props, well out of sight, may be needed to ensure that their long and transverse axes are parallel to the picture-plane. Early types of hand-axe may be nearly as thick as they are wide, so a small lens-aperture to give some depth of focus will be required, to ensure that all parts appear suitably sharp.

Lighting presents some problems. Great contrasts should be avoided since all details of workmanship may be lost in too deeply shaded areas. Diffused daylight often gives a suitably soft effect. If artificial light is used there should be counter-reflectors skilfully disposed to soften shadowed parts of particular pieces and the background may have to be specially lighted to throw up outlines of the pale-coloured specimens. Indeed, if the groups or some pieces are very pale, or even almost white in colour, it may be necessary to have a grey or even a really dark background to show them off properly.

Too soft an effect of top-lighting must, however, be avoided, for the object of the photograph is to show, if possible, every single flake-scar clearly outlined. Thus, moving lights during the exposure is on the whole not advisable, for by undue softening of what should appear as sharp edges and boundaries, a general loss of definition rather than any particular gain is likely to result. In a special case, on the other hand, it might achieve satisfactory effects unobtainable by other means, and so would be worth trying as an experiment, if results with static lighting did not come up to expectations.

METAL OBJECTS

These are often of varied colours and, if deeply corroded, may have rough, pock-marked or blistered surface-textures. In contrast with the case of the flint objects, such secondary surfaces are irrelevant to the originally manufactured shapes of the specimens and should not be emphasised by the lighting chosen.

If possible, pieces of similar material and quality only should appear in one photograph, i.e. not iron and bronze together, for instance, or some objects still covered with corrosion-products, as excavated, along with others cleaned and ready for exhibition. (The picture may, of course, be designed to demonstrate the effects of treatment for conservation and, in that case, objects 'before', 'during' and 'after' such treatment must be displayed together.) It may be hard, if the specimens in a single group are too diverse, to prescribe one lighting, background and exposure that will be ideal for all—better by far to treat them individually or in similar groups, if permissible.

The shadowless background obtained by laying out the objects on perspex over white paper would suit some subjects but not others. Red paper would give a dark background for pale objects. They should be raised by plasticine props about half-an-inch (12 mm) above its surface to ensure definition of their outlines. A dead black background is often very effective, but requires some experience in practice. Since the background is perfectly clear on the negative, some irradiation and greying of the edges of the image is often experienced during enlargement from it. This can be avoided only by shading the background during part of the exposure and is a matter of some skill and judgement. Plate 38 shows the beauty of an object displayed on a black background.

TEXTILES

Textiles make interesting subjects for photography, for both the variety of weaves and the colours in different patterns can be made to show up clearly, even in monochrome.

Oblique lighting is recommended, to accentuate relief and detail in shaded areas as well as in full light.

Whether a vertical or a horizontal attitude is chosen for the camera, the same kind of lighting is called for. In the former case the material, if not crumpled, will lie flat without fixing; in the latter it will have to be pinned on a board through the chosen background sheet. Such fixing will have to be by means of short headless panel pins, well pushed in so as to cast no shadows. Remember to include a suitable scale.

If any filter is used to differentiate by tone between different colours in the specimen itself, it will affect the colour of the background also, and this must be taken into account when making a choice of background-colour—i.e. quite early in preparing the subject. Neither by choice of filter nor in the selection of film or variation of development-time should too great a contrast result on the negative. Final differentiation between the various parts of the subject is best obtained by distinctive shading of them during the enlargement-exposure.

Both macro- and micro-photographs of parts of textile-subjects may be required for research purposes. These special techniques are described on p. 90–91.

COINS

The camera will be used in the vertical position. Coins require strong, oblique lighting to show up even low relief in good contrast, with little or no 'filling in' of shadows by reflection.

For those with left-facing heads, the light should fall on the coins from the right, as the features will be best accentuated by the shadows in this way. Should there be several in a group facing right also, discretion will have to be used to obtain the best, most uniform, effect, and this will perhaps be achieved by placing the light directly ahead, falling from the 'north' or near to it.

If a shadowless background is required, the group may be laid out on perspex, a white paper being positioned at a distance of six to eight inches (15–20 cms) behind it to avoid light-spread on to the faces of the coins. In the case of a dark background, the coins should be slightly raised above it on plasticine.

If a dead black background is used, both the obverse and reverse views of a group of coins may be shown on a single negative.

They are first laid out in vertical columns, each column having a space reserved to its right for the eventual reverse views. After the first exposure, the coins are turned over *sideways* to their right (if turned vertically the design would be inverted!) into the spaces provided, and the second exposure is then made. Great care must be taken to have columns and transverse rows quite straight and on the same lines in both positions. Nothing looks worse in a photograph than if the ranks are irregular or staggered. A small aperture is used, with an appropriately long exposure, to give the maximum definition.

As ever, a suitable scale must appear in the picture. It should be put in for the first exposure and be removed before the second. Quite apart from being over-exposed if left in both, it would almost inevitably be shifted out of its original position during re-arrangement of the coins and so give a double image.

Camera-shake during the exposures and, above all, any slight accidental shifting of the camera between exposures, must be avoided at all costs. Slight over-exposure and under-development results in a slightly softened negative, which is desirable.

White plaster casts of coins are best photographed with process-film or another very slow type. Process-film, as used for black-and-white line-work is recommended, but is available only as sheet-film, so would call for a stand- or field-camera with dark slides. Again, this should be over-exposed and under-developed to produce a soft negative with which contrast may be locally controlled in the printing.

If there is great variation in tone-colour in a group of coins to be photographed together, the images of individual pieces may be shaded during printing with a disc of cardboard mounted on a wire handle, and this will enable undue differences in tone to be evened out.

A more even effect is obtained if the darker pieces in a group can be positioned nearer to the light-source and *vice-versa*. A white scale should, similarly, be placed further from the light. In the case of clean silver or gold coins the best detail is shown by the use of polarised light to 'kill' intense high-lights and by using oblique diffused daylight for illumination.

X-RAY PHOTOGRAPHY

The use of X-rays sometimes enables structures to be photographed which lie beneath the surface of a body opaque to the visible wavelengths of light. Neither the longer infrared nor the shorter ultraviolet are of any use for this purpose.

Even the ultraviolet, from 4000 down to 500 ÅU (400–50 nm) has a much longer wavelength than X-rays, the 'softest' of which (least penetrating) begin at that lower limit. 'Hard' X-rays (more penetrating) have even shorter wavelengths.

As is well known, X-rays easily penetrate living soft tissues but are absorbed by bone and other mineral substances. Metals are especially opaque to X-rays, but if sufficiently thin and the radiation sufficiently hard even a metal object may show inequalities in different places, invisible at the surface but photographable on film. Such would be, for instance, areas with silver-inlay decoration on an iron sword covered with rust.

X-ray pictures unlike photographs are not images formed by a lens but shadow-pictures (skiagrams (Gr.)) showing differences in density, to the radiation, of an object interposed between the X-ray tube and the sensitive film. Thus a bullet (metal) lying in soft tissue by the shaft of a human leg-bone will be represented in an X-ray picture by a deep, sharply-defined shadow near the less evenly dense bone-shadow within a scarcely-at-all shadowed outline of the leg. (In fact skiagrams are seldom printed but are interpreted from the negative, on which, of course, shadows appear pale and areas much affected by the transmitted radiation dark.)

The increase of penetration of solids by X-rays depends on their decreasing wavelength—'soft' or long wavelength/'hard' or short wavelength. The wavelength of the X-rays emitted by a tube in turn depends on the energy of the electron-stream striking the target which emits the X-rays and this again on the high-voltage electric potential used to accelerate them. 'Soft' X-rays are produced by H.T. potentials of 10–20 kV and have a wavelength of perhaps 1 ÅU (0·1 nm). Their

82

intensity is expressed in milliampères (mA), their 'hardness' in terms of kilovolts (kV).

As in ordinary photography, the distance between target and film and exposure times giving satisfactory skiagrams of different objects must be recorded and used as precedents to estimate requirements of unknowns. Exposures of a few seconds are sufficient for thin metal objects under the soft X-rays given above. 100kV (hard) radiation would be required for thicker objects.

X-ray film is coated on *both* sides with the silver-halide emulsion to increase its sensitivity.

Development is important in the production of a good picture. Long development increases contrast but this will not be necessary for every subject. As in photographic processing, proper records of development times and temperatures which yielded satisfactory negatives will pay off handsomely in reduction of wastage when undertaking a new subject.

X-ray equipment when in use is a source of radiation extremely dangerous to health and exposure to it must be avoided. There are perfectly adequate known simple precautions which are scrupulously observed by all trained operators. No one should attempt to use X-rays without experience and proper tuition, with the strictest supervision in the early stages.

THE DARKROOM

Whether it is a temporary darkroom on an excavation-site, or one to be permanently situated at the home-base that we are designing, the advance planning of it is of the greatest importance, for it is here that the products of all the preceding careful work in the field will be completed, and, indeed, improved if they are unavoidably imperfect owing to unfavourable conditions out-of-doors.

A satisfactory *field-darkroom* may be prefabricated in wooden sections to be assembled on the site. When erected, this forms a small box-like room, if need be but a few feet each way in dimensions, though slightly more commodious quarters might be of advantage and not too expensive. In rainy climates it must, however modest in size, be completely weatherproof. In dry it should, above all, resist wind and the entry of dust. In any event it must provide perfect darkness, so that the first test will have to be for light-tightness and any chinks discovered after assembly be sealed at once with self-adhesive drafting tape or other suitable opaque material.

Two shelves at waist-level are required: one for materials and equipment, the other for processing. These may be carried loose and be designed to slot into the walls and there be firmly supported on struts. A shutter-section, light-tight when closed, should be included, with a loose sheet of perspex, fitting into grooves on either side inside it, for a window. Internal light would be provided by an alternative pair of battery-powered lamps controlled by a two-way switch, one being equipped with a safe-light filter, the open light being for use in contact-printing.

Both door and shutter should, for safety, be lockable or bolted, on the *inside* (as well as from without), to prevent their being thoughtlessly opened by anybody outside during processing. Some built-in ventilation (light-tight!) would be of advantage, especially in a hot climate, though, with a small darkroom-hut, opening the door at intervals, between operations requiring darkness, would otherwise sufficiently clear the air.

A shady situation for the hut in the first place would be advisable, thus at once excluding both excessive light and heat. The latter consideration is especially important in the tropics, where avoidably high temperatures would unnecessarily affect processing.

Where there are existing buildings sufficiently near the excavation, a wine-cellar, for instance, would afford a suitably dark and cool photographic laboratory almost without further adaptation, but such civilised luxuries cannot often be relied on and the portable hut is indispensable in most wildernesses. One might nevertheless hopefully include a corkscrew among one's photographic impedimenta, in addition to the bottle-opener which every experienced field worker carries as a matter of course!

The *professional laboratory*, built and/or equipped to the photographer's own specification, should include maximum facilities for simplifying every kind of work to be carried out in it.

One should make a point, before taking major planning decisions, of visiting comparable studios to see how others have employed modern methods in their approach to common problems and to profit by their experience, whether favourable or otherwise, of such innovations.

Whatever the space available and whether the darkroom and studio are to be combined in one room or kept separate, some basic considerations of design will remain unchanged.

Ventilation. The darkroom must have a window which can be opened at intervals to admit daylight and air, thus facilitating cleaning and ventilation. This window, when shut, is simply and quickly blacked out by means of a dark blind running in lateral grooves. When dark, the room should be ventilated by a light-tight extractor-fan to maintain comfortable working conditions.

84

Lighting. Internal lighting will be by safelights, strategically placed, which, by means of a two-way switch, can be exchanged for a central general white light.

Sinks. They should be as spacious and as accessible as possible, preferably free-standing, to be reached quickly from any of the surrounding wall-benches, but at such a distance from them as to avoid accidental splashes in dry areas. If wall-mounted, they should be strictly separated, if not screened off, from adjacent dry work-benches. Where space is restricted, however, they may have removable wooden covers to afford dry working areas when not in use for wet processing. Both hot and cold water services are desirable, the respective taps being clearly distinguishable by touch or in subdued light.

Benches for enlargers should be of a convenient height and, if the studio and darkroom are combined, have drawers under them which are light-tight, for easy access to sensitive papers and films, the stocks of which currently in use will be kept there.

There should be plenty of electricity points at convenient positions so that enlargers and other pieces of equipment may easily be plugged in wherever they may be needed. The final best siting of safe-lights will depend on the arrangement of the processing facilities.

If there is a separate studio, windows there for admitting daylight are very desirable. These should be individually controllable by blinds so as to gain the utmost flexibility as, for instance, for oblique lighting effects. A bench below the windows, for sorting or mounting prints in good light, should have knee-holes at intervals so that one or more people can work sitting at it. Cupboards and/or drawers under this bench will be useful for storage of small equipment and materials of all kinds.

Free-standing folding tables are useful for setting up groups of objects for photography whether in artificial or daylight. They should have vertical background-boards which can be fitted as required.

When planning the layout, space must be allowed for all other requirements. Among these will be a negative-loading room which need be no larger than a tele-phone-booth. This should be fitted with a shelf at hand-height when standing and a perfectly light-tight door which can be locked, bolted or latched *from the inside*, to prevent unforeseen intrusion when it is in use. Even a red warning-light, switched automatically by closing the door, showing that the loading room is occupied, cannot absolutely prevent accidental interference. Locking cupboards with shelves, if not a separate small room, must be provided for stocks in hand, and there will have to be space allotted for drying films, glazing prints or dry-mounting if these operations are mechanised or need special installations.

Detailed scale-drawings at the planning stage will help to eliminate possible faults, omissions or drawbacks in design which would be much more difficult to remedy if they were allowed first to become actualities.

Chapter ten – Special techniques

INFRARED PHOTOGRAPHY

Whether a 5″×4″ plate-camera or a 35 mm miniature is to be used, a separate field-case or bag should be kept ready-packed with the necessary equipment. A red filter will be needed for visual focusing, an infrared filter (generally the 88A) and the special infrared sensitive film or plates. If the latter are packed in a black polythene bag, this will prevent fogging or deterioration of the emulsion on standing.

Plates should not be loaded until they are needed for use, for they may become marked in the slide by repeated vibration or movement or fogged by exposure to heat.

The exposures given by a meter-reading taken without the filter may safely be multiplied by a factor of ×4 to ×6 when the 88A filter is in use, without risk of over-exposure. A hot sun beating on the subject, as is often the case in the Middle East, or the presence of heat-haze, will demand a somewhat reduced exposure, and this will call for experience and judgement to make a correct adjustment.

The emulsion of 35 mm film tends to be much slower than that of plates. Exposure-times will have to be greatly increased to allow for this. Like the plates, infrared sensitive film is easily marked by friction or mechanical stress. Avoid pulling it too tightly over the rollers when loading.

It is advisable to develop infrared materials as soon as possible after exposing (Development, p. 44).

An exposure made of the same subject on ordinary panchromatic film makes an interesting comparison with infrared work.

Photography of small objects under infrared radiation may on occasion be useful, since it may show up detail which is invisible in ordinary light using panchromatic film.

Preliminary experiments with varying exposures of the infrared material to be

87

used should have been carried out at leisure in the darkroom at the home base and the results, at various apertures and with the appropriate exposure-times, have been noted. There may be no time or adequate opportunity for experiment in the field, where the snap use of infrared (or ultraviolet) may mean the difference between success and failure in obtaining a satisfactory record of some possibly evanescent feature.

The camera must first be loaded with infrared-sensitive film or plate. A 250–1000 watt battery-driven flash-lamp, emitting radiation in the 700–900 nm band, will give a spectral distribution similar to that of photofloods and be satisfactory in the infrared range. Infrared filters are obtainable to cover the flash, but it is far more effective to fit a filter over the camera-lens itself, thus excluding all visible light during the exposure. This filter should be a deep red, 88A, or even, 25A. This last should, in any case, be used to obtain a sharp focus by eye, the deep red being in the visible waveband nearest to the infra-red by which the effective exposure will be made, but, even so, this focus cannot, by its nature, be absolutely accurate and the smallest practicable aperture—$f.32$ or $f.45$—should be used to give the maximum depth of focus and so satisfactory sharpness of the invisible infrared image.

Infrared-sensitive film, used without the special filter, will give results comparable with ordinary panchromatic material.

There are many uses for infrared monochrome photography in the field. One of the most outstanding is for penetrating mist in distant views. The relatively long visible waves at the red end of the spectrum, and, even more so, the still longer-wavelength infrared radiation, beyond the range which the eye can appreciate, are much less scattered by water-vapour, haze or mist-droplets in the atmosphere than the short blue and ultraviolet. As a result, a scene which, to the eye, is more or less obscured by mist or fog may appear very much clearer on an infrared-sensitive negative.

Special fine-grain development (p. 44) is essential for infrared film. Otherwise undue 'graininess' may interfere with the reproduction of fine detail in the picture.

INFRARED COLOUR PHOTOGRAPHY

The 'false-colour' infrared technique is much used nowadays in aerial photography to show differences in infrared absorptive and reflective properties of vegetation, water, bare soil, buildings and so on in the field of view. After processing, these are rendered on the finished transparency or print in visible colours which bear no relation to their natural colours, but are very distinctive. Thus, healthy green vegetation appears in clear, bright reds, while diseased or wilted

88

plants and trees show only a dull pink, a dirty red or even grey. Water comes out in vivid blues, roads and buildings in white, grey or mauve, according to the materials of which they are made. Such pictures are of value to geologists, foresters, agriculturalists and ecologists. Their possibilities in the archaeological field so far remain relatively untried, though the evidence of crop and soil-marks covering antiquities in agricultural land would evidently emerge still more clearly than they do in ordinary light.

Soil-horizons, rock stratification and the varying humanly-formed levels in an archaeological section may be made more clearly distinguishable in even a monochrome infrared photograph than by any means using only the ordinary visible wavelengths. The method is at least worth trying in difficult cases.

Infrared colour-film is not difficult to use in the field after some experiment. The time of day and character of the visible light will affect the intensity of infrared reflection from the subject. These details, together with those of aperture and exposure, must be recorded for each picture. A yellow filter should always be used to cut out radiation at the blue end of the spectrum.

The most difficult thing to memorise is the natural colours in the subject that the eye sees and those corresponding to their infrared reflection as recorded by the infrared emulsion. It would be instructive to study side by side ordinary colour-transparencies taken at the same time as those on infrared sensitive colour-film and to note the characteristic differences. These depend on the differential absorption and reflection of visible and infrared radiation wavebands by different objects in the field of view—such differences being sometimes, indeed, dependent on their particular chemical constitution.

Green plants afford a case in point. Their visible greenness is due to their content of the pigment chlorophyll, which absorbs the energy of the red and orange-yellow wavebands contained in daylight to promote photosynthetic chemical reactions necessary to the life of the plant. Chlorophyll reflects radiation in the green waveband. As shades of green reflectivity in nature vary widely, so do the absorptive capacities of the respective plant-leaves, the infrared colour photographs are capable of showing vivid contrasts between different plant species in an assemblage. Areas of dead or diseased foliage in a group of a single species might also be clearly apparent.

The infrared colour-emulsion renders differences in wavelength within the infrared waveband as differences in *visible* colour, i.e. 'transposes' the invisible infrared scale into a different 'key' (to use a musical analogy) in the visible range.

The following table is a useful reminder of the actual changes in colour-rendering corresponding to the visible and infrared scales:

Visual appearance	Infrared absorbed	Infrared reflected
Red	Green	Yellow
Green	Blue	Magenta
Blue	Grey to black	Red
Cyan	Blue	Magenta
Magenta	Green	Yellow
Yellow	Cyan	Grey to white
Grey	Cyan	Grey

Correct development of infrared sensitive colour-emulsions is essential to success. They can only be properly processed by the makers.

PHOTO-MACROGRAPHY

This is a technique for photographing fine detail of a larger subject, or a very small entire object, in close-up, at some degree of relatively low magnification. It differs from photo-micrography (see below) in that the ordinary camera-lens is used, while in the latter the image is formed by the optical equipment of a compound microscope, so that much higher magnifications are possible.

The 35 mm camera equipped with its normal lens of 50 mm focal length has a near working-distance of acceptable sharpness of the image with the object positioned at a distance of about 3 ft (1 m). Image-sharpness at any closer approach of the camera (increased size of image) requires extension of the lens correspondingly beyond its normal distance from the focal plane. This is achieved by interposing extension-rings (p. 6) or a continuously-extensible bellows (p. 6) between the normal lens-mounting and the base of the lens.

When the distances between lens and object and lens and film are equal, the relative dimensions of the image and the object will be 1 : 1 (life size). As the lens is approached still more nearly to the object, the distance between lens and focal plane will have to be made greater than the working distance and the image will be magnified, as in an enlarger or slide-projector. There are obvious practical limits to this process, principally of adequate lighting of the object, sufficient width of field of view and especially of depth of field, in the case of objects having appreciable modelling and relief, all of which does not lie in one plane. This will be the case even if very small lens-apertures are used. Magnifications of about ×5 linear (5 : 1) are close to the practical limits. An exceedingly rigid mount for

90

the camera and lens-extension and the utmost ingenuity and care are required for success, even so.

PHOTO-MICROGRAPHY

Recording photographically the often highly-magnified image formed by the compound microscope depends entirely on the optics of the microscope itself. The ordinary camera-lens is removed and the camera-body with the film in position is firmly mounted in the optical axis of the microscope to receive, on exposure, the real image, projected beyond the ocular, of the object on the stage.

Magnifications obtainable with most microscope objective and eyepiece combinations vary between $\times 10$ and $\times 1000$. The quality of the image depends on that of the instrument and the manipulative skills of a microscopist, rather than of a photographer.

Microscopic objects for the light-microscope have to be quite flat—thin sections of transparent materials viewed by transmitted light or, for those which are opaque, such as metals, a polished and perhaps chemically-etched plane surface, seen by reflected light. At any but the lowest attainable magnifications there is practically no depth of field at all.

Correct exposure is found either by trial and error or by the use of a special photo-electric cell of greater sensitivity than that used in the field. Once again: correct judgement may be developed by practice, or by the S.E.1 photometer held directly against the ground glass screen.

Black-and-white photomicrographs are adequate for many purposes, but colour-photography has greatly increased their usefulness in some fields. Many microscopic preparations are positively beautiful, seen in colour, as well as more informative than monochromes. The only drawback to colour-photos is the great expense of reproducing them in printers' inks! In the archaeological field, the consulting natural scientist and the conservator will be the chief users of photo-micrography.

Unless the microscope itself is very rigid and its focusing rack-work unworn and stiff, only the very lightest camera body can be attached and be entirely supported by it with any satisfaction. Generally it is better to have a separate pillar-support and adjustable sliding collar to hold the camera-mounting vertically over the microscope, with a bellows or a simple black-cloth tube held by rubber bands between the eyepiece and the camera-front to exclude extraneous light. Focusing is on the ground-glass screen of the field camera or in the case of a miniature camera, a through-the-lens reflex viewfinder is essential.

Type of microscopes are legion. Most are designed to examine thin specimens or sections mounted on 3"×1" glass slides by transmitted light at fairly high magnifications. These are held on a stage beneath which is a more or less complicated arrangement of filter, iris-diaphragm and focusing, centring condenser for concentrating the available light into a uniform pencil of rays just to fill the aperture of the objective in use. There is, consequently, only a relatively short working distance generally provided. For our purpose low-power objectives (×5, ×10) with correspondingly long working distances are needed and since we are to use reflected, not transmitted, light the substage equipment is all superfluous.

A low-power (×5 to ×50) binocular microscope with the camera mounted above one ocular is probably the best equipment, having a long working distance and usually no stage or substage. They are generally mounted on their own vertical pillars and horizontal arms and so are freely adjustable to focus on the surface even of a thick object such as an entire pot or wide one like a brick or a tile. The magnification of the image as seen by eye at the standard tube length of 160 mm, is that of the objective (say ×5) multiplied by that of the ocular (say ×4), i.e. ×20. At any larger distance, such as with a longer tube-length or at the focal plane of the camera mounted over the ocular, the magnification will be somewhat greater. At low magnifications, direct measurement of the field of view and of the image with dividers, screw-callipers, slide-gauges or such-like, may be possible to determine the exact magnification or to adjust it to a round figure— ×10, ×20, etc. With higher powers, an eyepiece-graticule will be needed for this purpose, its subdivisions previously calibrated by means of a stage micrometer viewed at the same working-distance as the eventual subject.

Lighting for episcopic work will depend on the nature of the subject. For faint tool marks, signs of wear on flint implements, shallow incised or stamped devices or decorations, the light should be intense, falling on the surface of the object from a low angle so as to cast a pronounced shadow emphasising the detail. A low-voltage microscope-lamp, working from a mains transformer, equipped with a focusing lens and field-iris to control the width and intensity of the beam, will ordinarily serve, but on occasion a 'Pointolite' enclosed arc-lamp or a multi-filament lamp in a suitable housing may be needed to give sufficient light for a reasonably short exposure in the case of a rough-textured or dark-coloured object. Exposures will have to be found by experiment.

At magnifications even as low as ×10 there will be little depth of field. If the part of the subject in the field of view is not fairly flat it will be found difficult to bring all of it simultaneously to an acceptably sharp focus. Since the microscope is not normally provided with a diaphragm, it may be necessary to devise one to restrict its working aperture. A small disc of black paper with a central perforation may be inserted behind the back lens of the objective and this may appreciably improve the depth of focus, but, evidently will call either for higher-powered illumination or a greatly increased exposure time. Experiment and ingenuity to improvise will generally yield satisfactory results even in difficult cases.

A polarising filter before the lamp may be used to suppress unwanted reflections. A vertical illuminator, as used in metallography, to pass a beam of light on to an opaque object through the objective lens itself, may be useful on occasion, but is incapable of showing differences in relief—it is like taking a photograph in the field with the sun directly behind the camera: flat and shadowless lighting. If there is a colour-contrast in the object this may be the method of choice.

Low-power photomicrography by transmitted light of transparent or translucent subjects presents certain difficulties—mainly of uniform lighting of a larger field of view than those for which most ordinary microscopes are designed. The principle to be borne in mind is that the substage-condenser should always be of a focal length double that of the objective in use—2″ for 1″ objective, 4″ for a 2″, and so on. This may call for more space in the substage between condenser and object than is normally available. In that case, if the existing condenser is removed, the wide parallel beam from a free-standing long-focus condenser between lamp and microscope may be thrown on to the plane mirror and so be reflected up the optic axis of the microscope.

Whatever the lighting arrangements, it is important for obtaining a crisp, uniformly lit image in transmitted light that the beam from the condenser should fully and evenly fill the front lens of the objective, *but no more*. Any peripheral light beyond this must be cut out by means of the substage iris or it will cause 'glare' and spoil the contrast of the image. Direct incident light (on the front of the object), due to general lighting of the room or to unwanted reflections from the instruments, will also detract from contrast. Final focusing and exposure are therefore best carried out in darkness save for the minimum beam necessary to full illumination of the object. Low-power microscope work on rocks, minerals, or other anisotropic materials (e.g. cellulose fibres), using 'crossed' polars, is greatly assisted by the use of polarising filters.

Polarising filters (or Nicol prisms) pass light-rays vibrating in one plane only. If two such filters are 'crossed' (placed so that the planes in which they respectively pass light are at right-angles), no light at all passes. If an anisotropic transparent body (such as a mineral crystal, which is itself capable of polarising the light-beam) is now inserted between them, it will rotate the plane of polarisation of the light to some degree, so that this part of the light will be transmitted by the upper polar and the anisotropic object appear more or less brightly lit on a dark background.

Instead of the old-style Nicol prism in the substage, a piece of sheet Polaroid may be placed as polariser in front of the lamp or long-focus condenser. Another, the analyser, may be positioned above the eyepiece, in front of the camera, if the microscope tube is not provided with a slot for it. Crossed polars absorb some 9/10th of the light that would pass through the object without them, so that the exposure in polarised light may require to be as much as 10 times as long as in ordinary light. This is a useful rule-of-thumb, for experimenting, but will vary with the degree of optical activity and orientation of the specimen.

LANTERN-SLIDES

Standard 2″×2″ slides for projection may be made from positive or negative film, both in colour and in black-and-white.

Coloured positive transparencies (diapositives) are produced direct from the miniature film exposed in the camera (Kodachrome, Agfachrome, Ilford Colour). Colour negative-type films (Ektachrome, Kodacolor) yield first a negative from which either transparencies or paper prints are indirectly obtained. In the former case the price of the unexposed film includes processing; in the latter, processing is separately charged.

For black-and-white slides, the same negative used for making paper prints may be used to print (by reduction or contact) on to slow-speed film which can be processed under subdued darkroom lighting. In the case of 35 mm negatives, single frames or whole strips may be printed direct on to film as one would expose a contact-print. Contrast can be controlled in the developing process.

Black-and-white reversal film, in which the negative image first obtained on exposure is reversed during processing of the material, is easily managed at home, following the directions given, and is also widely used for making slides. Dia-Direct is one such material, the processing of which is carried out by the manufacturer.

Slides should always be mounted for use between cover-glasses, whether in ready-made plastic frames or by the passe-partout method, using self-adhesive tape. This protects the emulsion from dirt and from accidental scratches during handling

94

and avoids loss of focus during projection by buckling of the emulsion when exposed to the heat from the lamp.

COPYING

Line drawings or plans may have to be copied in the field-studio. Since a regular studio copying stand is unlikely to be available, the work will have to be done either with the field-camera or a miniature mounted on the tripod, the subject being pinned out on a drawing-board or other convenient flat surface. Both the camera and the plane of the subject being movable, the principal requirement is to adjust them, not only with the image correctly centred but with the subject plane and focal plane strictly parallel. Any deviation from parallelism will introduce distortion of scale in different areas of the subject, even if overall sharpness of focus is unaffected,

The field-camera is probably to be preferred, the larger format of the negative ensuring recording of even the finest detail. With due care in exposing and processing, however, even the miniature-sized negative will reproduce satisfactorily.

Whatever lens is used, it should have a flat field and give an image equally sharp all over. This calls for accurate focusing and the use of a relatively small aperture to reduce aberrations.

Process sheet-film (p. 37), suitable for reproduction of line-drawings are the material of choice for single exposures with the field-camera. They are obtainable in a variety of sizes. For the miniature, similar material is available as panchromatic roll-film with a speed of 50 Weston, and this gives excellent results.

If a drawing includes coloured, as well as black lines, these should clearly register a tone contrasting with the black. Using panchromatic film and a green filter, a pale red line will be darkened to contrast with the white paper but not so much as to appear in full black. If ortho-material is used (as is sometimes advised), not being red-sensitive, the line will be clean white on the negative, full black on the print, and so not be distinguishable from the originally black lines.

The slow panchromatic emulsion (ASA or Weston 50) renders the fine detail by enabling weak lines to build up somewhat on the negative during the relatively long exposure.

Processing, too, is important. A satisfactory negative will probably be obtained at the first attempt if the recommended time/temperature scale for the particular developer is adhered to. Identical results are more easily obtained in making several copies of line-work than for half-tones, which may vary considerably in tone from print to print unless great care is exercised over exposures and processing times.

Prints or enlargements for reproduction must show good detail in all tones, and clean, distinct lines for line-drawings. In the latter case, if two adjacent fine lines merge in the photograph they will reproduce on the block as only one.

For half-tone work, differences in tone or colour appreciable in the original or negative must be faithfully rendered in the print. The techniques applied to differentiate strata in an archaeological section in the field may be employed here also—by choice of appropriate filters. Wrong exposure or development or the use of an unsuitable grade of printing paper may cause areas of distinct tone in the original negative to merge in the print.

If there is any doubt about one's own printing technique, it is preferable for reproduction to have a first-class print professionally made to render all the detail which the artist or photographer has put into the drawing or negative. The ideal print for reproduction is on glossy paper, well glazed, in $8\frac{1}{2}''\times6\frac{1}{2}''$ format ($21\cdot5\times16\cdot5$ cm) or larger.

Some blockmakers prefer to make their own prints from the negative, if it is available.

The half-tone screens used by blockmakers are of varying fineness; so are the grades of paper used in book-production, and both will affect the quality of the eventual line- or half-tone print. The finer the screen and the smoother-surfaced the paper used for the printed plate the better will be the reproduction of fine detail present in the original—also the greater the expense on both scores!

For newspaper photographs, to be printed on cheap paper, the blockmaker uses a coarse screen of which the 'grain' is readily visible to the naked eye. This is suitable only for half-tone work without much detail. A medium screen would be used for illustrations in a book with good quality paper priced at 2–3 gns. Half-tones to be printed on glossy art paper would call for a fine screen of 120 or more lines to the inch, which would reproduce very fine detail, but be proportionately more expensive.

Appendix – Common Faults

COMMON FAULTS	LIKELY CAUSES
Image out of focus	Camera too near to object. Lens incorrectly focused for the working-distance.
Thin negative	Exposure not sufficient or development incomplete.
Dense negative	Over exposure or overdevelopment.
Dark streaks on negative	Fog, light entering camera, or stress-marks, faulty dark slide, bellows perforated, anti-reflection paint worn.
Uneven patches on negative	Uneven development or fixing.
Drying marks on negative/ or a wetting agent	Negative moved while drying, or hard water used for washing. Distilled water for the final rinse prevents drying marks.
Finger marks	Handling negative with warm hands while loading film or preparing for processing.
White spots on negative	Negative not agitated during development. Air bubbles cause these marks, or dust on the film.
Cut off	Faulty lens hood or excessive rising front of a field camera.
Reticulation	When negative is removed from a solution at a high temperature into a much cooler one.
Converging parallel lines	Failure to maintain film in a vertical plane.
Halation	Light passing through film and being reflected from film or glass back. A special backing is now used on films to prevent this.

Melting of emulsion	Drying or developing at too high a temperature.
Parallax, resulting in cutting off some area of the negative when a close-up is taken	With a twin-lens camera, the viewing lens is in a different viewing-position from that of the taking lens. (Remedy: to allow for this either by being content with a slightly smaller image, or by centring on a point on the object at the same distance above the true centre as that of the viewing lens is above the taking lens.)
Reversal of negative	Stray light fogging the unexposed areas of the film during development so that the image comes out partly negative, partly positive, or gross over-exposure.
Under-exposed negative	Intensifying chemical solution obtainable for redeveloping.
Over-exposed negative	Chemical solution obtainable for reducing.

Conclusion

Successful archaeological photography is the outcome (apart from the occasional unrepeatable 'fluke'!) of adequate forethought and planning before even loading a camera, of unhurried consideration of each subject, of common sense and inventiveness in the application of simple theory to the problems in hand, of scrupulous care at every stage (in the knowledge that a bad print can undo all the skill that went into making a good negative), of a little luck and of the experience that obtains an adequate result when even that fails!

It is to be hoped that the practical experience of one photographer, embodied in this book, may help others to avoid perpetuating some of the mistakes which we all make at least once in our time!

Plates

1 The field camera: double dark slides, roll film back, interchangeable lens panel, filters and Weston light meter.

2 Sanderson, or Technical, field camera: interchangeable lenses, lens hood, filters, roll film back.

3   Zeiss hand-stand: single film holders, roll film back, filters and Weston light meter.

4   35 mm miniature camera: interchangeable lens, filters, electronic flash, Weston light meter.

5   Paillard Bolex cine camera.

6   Paillard Bolex cine camera.
mechanism.

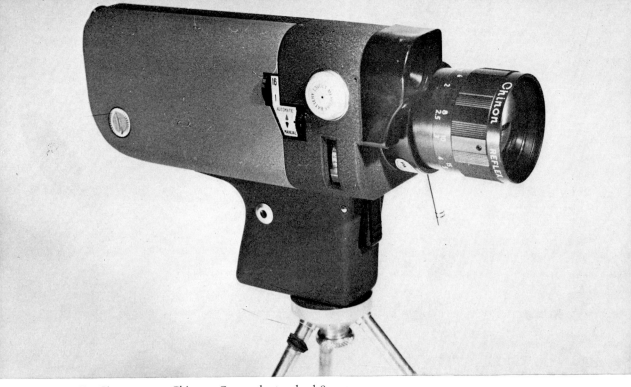

7 Cine camera: Chinnon-Concord, standard 8 mm

8 Cloud formation emphasised by the use of a red filter and panchromatic film to darken the blue sky. The filter also makes the green leaves black—a dramatic contrast.

9 Views of St Alphage, London Wall, taken from the same position with a change of the focal length of the lens, using a 35 mm camera: (a) 35 mm wide-angle lens;

(b) 50 mm lens;

(c) 135 mm telephoto lens.

10
St Mary's, Aldermanbury, underground tomb;
(a) in natural light. Very little detail is visible in the shadows. Even if a single flash only were used the exterior would also be more brightly lit and the result would still be too contrasty, as it is here.

(b) evening light (oblique) enabled a time exposure to be made with the use of intermittent flashes from different angles to penetrate the shadows. The 5×4 format was used, aperture stopped down to ƒ.45 to enable a prolonged exposure. Developed in Kodak Time Standard Developer for 8 minutes.

11
Fragment of linen textile in a museum case, University College; (a) using 35 mm camera, aperture ƒ.22, exposure 30 seconds in poor natural daylight. The shadow was caused by the metal cornerpiece of the showcase.

(b) from the same negative as (a). The unwanted shadow was eliminated during the enlargement-exposure by shading out the under-lighted negative image of the shadow with a pencil.

12
Yarnbury hill-fort, Wiltshire. (a) the 35 mm wide-angle lens was used with FP4 film. Exposure: 1/30th second at *f*.11. Shows the full-scale and extent of this Iron Age fortification.

(b) using the 135 mm tele-photo lens fitted with a red filter and a lens hood. The latter also served to protect the lens from rain drops. Aperture *f*.4, 1/30th second exposure. Brings the central features within sight in reasonable detail but, with this narrower field, fails to show that it is only part of a much larger whole.

13

Walbury hill camp, Berkshire.
(a) photographed with the 35 mm camera, 50 mm lens, FP4 film, aperture ƒ.11, 1/60th second; shows contrast between the slight outer slope of the ditch and the inner, steeper slope to the summit of the bank, and this last is better seen against a temporary lightening of the sky behind it.

(b) from near the ditch-bottom, shows the true ditch-profile more clearly but has an uninteresting foreground. These two views were taken within a few yards of each other.

Note to 12 and 13. Photographed with 35 mm camera in pouring rain, mist and wind. During the half-hour spent on the sites periods of waiting were necessary for the rain-mist on the horizon to move so that the contours of the subject could be clearly seen. Absence of radiation from the sun made infrared photography useless in these instances. Patience, the friend of all archaeologists, enabled satisfactory results to be obtained.

14 Maiden Castle, Dorset. By choosing exactly the right moment, the strong oblique light
is made to define, not only the opposing slopes, but the horizontal surface of the fill
between them. The two figures give the true scale. (M. B. Cookson)

15

(a) and (b) these were two pictures from the same point on the Chagford–Two Bridges road across Dartmoor. One at about midday and the other towards sunset with very oblique light. View approximately westward; August–September. What show up are traces of previous cultivation (medieval ridge-and-furrow), the land now having been abandoned so far as agriculture is concerned. Camera 35 mm, exposure by Weston meter reading, film FP4. (E. Pyddoke)

16
Stanwick. The light comes from behind the trees towards the camera outlining the summit of the bank against their shadow. This is repeated in the shadows cast by the end of the rampart where it abuts on the track-way in the foreground. Half-plate camera, panchromatic film. (M. B. Cookson)

17
Stanwick. The light comes towards the camera from half-right ahead, casting deep shadows into the grid-squares. The full lighted near sides of each square are cleanly silhouetted against them. Half-plate camera, 203 mm lens, panchromatic film. (M. B. Cookson)

18 Stanwick. A high, slightly diffused sun throws enough shadow to give relief to the ditch cut into well-bedded limestone, to the restored dry masonry of the revetted scarp and even to the section through the filling on the left. Half-plate camera, panchromatic film. (M. B. Cookson)

19 (a), (b), (c) and (d). Panoramic view of a site. The two photographs (a) and (b), were taken from the same viewpoint successively of two fields of view on the site, using a 35 mm miniature camera fitted with the normal 50 mm focal length lens. There is a small overlap in their fields. With the left half overlapping the right, (c), so as to match up the details together as well as possible, from the middle of the height, upwards and downwards, a cut with a sharp knife was made through both prints, exactly at the midpoint of the overlap. When now joined edge-to-edge the cut prints represent the whole scene adequately. The slight distortion seen where, for instance, the cut bisects the second hypocaust-pillar from the far end is due to contrary lens-aberrations near the margins of each field of view. Join-displaying only insignificant and, indeed, impercept-ible aberrations at the cuts would have been obtained if *three* overlapping views had been available, not two only, so that only one-third of each print had been used.

20

Silbury Hill, Wiltshire.

(a) photographed with the light coming from behind the mound. This is a usually successful technique for giving a good outline and showing relief. The vast size of the monument swallows up the details of the mound and the result is uninteresting.

(b) with a side light on the mound various details of the earthwork show up well, for instance the slight hollow near the top was scarcely visible in (a).

The red filter used in (b) makes the picture even more striking by distinguishing the clouds. 35 mm camera, Ilford FP4 film, aperture 22, exposure Weston meter reading and for (b) ×3 for red filter.

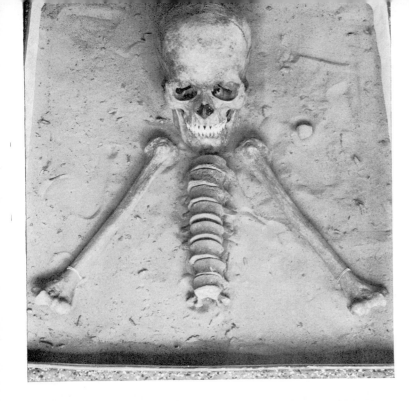

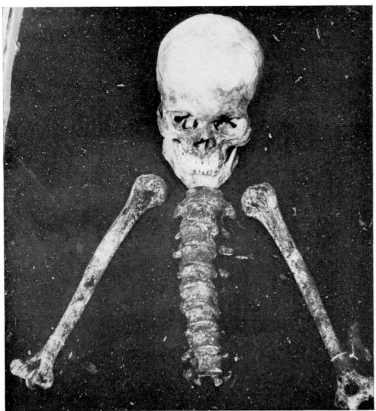

21

(a) and (b) experimental layout of skull and bones on sand; in both cases a 5×4 camera with 203 mm lens was used. For (a) aperture ƒ.32, panchromatic film. 10 seconds exposure, lighting by two 150 watt lamps, one on either side, developed in Kodak Time Standard Developer for 10 minutes. For (b) aperture ƒ.11, 2B filter, Ilford Zenith plate; pair of ultraviolet battery lamps used, one on either side; exposure 15 minutes; developed in Kodak Time Standard Developer for 20 minutes (twice normal time). Fluorescence brings out different surface-detail from that shown in ordinary light.

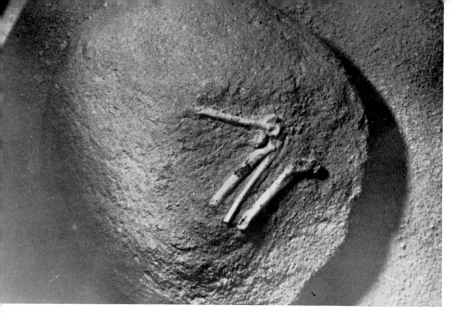

22
Using 35 mm camera, 50 mm lens, in

(a) panchromatic film; bones slightly concealed by sand, lighting by diffused daylight; in (b) 2B filter, aperture ƒ.11 illuminated by UV battery lamp for 2 minutes on either side. Kodak recording film, 1000 Weston. The bones fluoresced; some which were not visible under normal light were revealed. This technique when raising skeletons from sand soil may easily provide a record of what might otherwise be destroyed. An improvised black-out tent was used. Unfortunately only the 50 mm lens was available, instead of a wide-angle which would have given a large image on the negative.

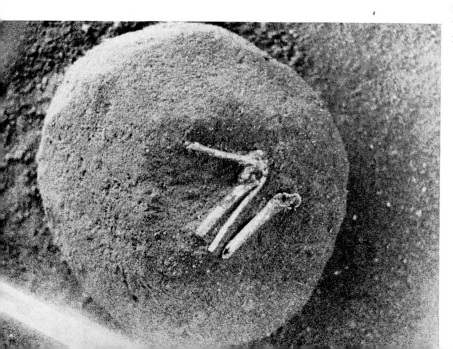

23 Battery-powered ultraviolet lamp, giving radiation in the longer UV waveband (365 mm) costing approximately £15. Replacements for the battery may be obtained in any country overseas. Size: 10×8 (254×204 mm); weight 7 lb. (3.2 kilos).

24

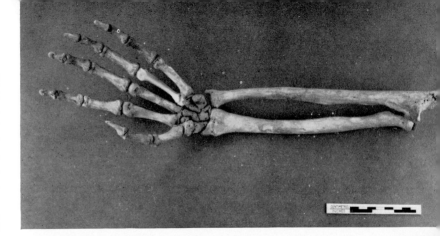

Human remains from Grasswell Priory. (a) and (b) reconstructed human left hand and forearm from a reliquary, severed from the upper arm at the elbow joint by a heavy sharp implement such as an axe. The 4th metacarpal is a cast in plastic. Photographed on a Gandolfi 5×4 camera, 203 mm lens.

(a) aperture ƒ.32, panchromatic film. Developed in Kodak Time Standard Developer for 10 minutes.

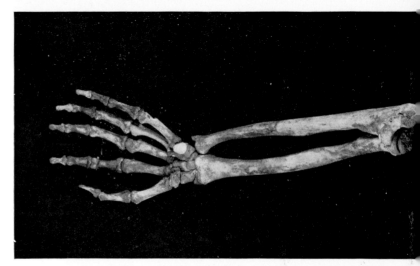

(b) photographed by fluorescence under ultraviolet radiation, 2B filter, Kodak Ortho Royal Film, aperture ƒ.22, exposure 30 minutes. Developed in Kodak Time Standard Developer for 20 minutes, twice the normal developing time, as recommended for the specialised work. The fluorescence of the bone shows the modelling at the joints extremely well. Artifacts are exposed—the two ungual phalanges of the fourth and fifth fingers, whittled in wood, and the pisiform bone, modelled in plasticine, for the restoration. The artificiality of the fourth metacarpal is not so evident here as in (a). The contrast created by ultraviolet greatly improves detail.

(c) 5×4 camera, 6½ inch lens, panchromatic film, aperture ƒ.32. 150 watt lamp in reflector was moved about during exposure. It was directed obliquely from the right to light the cut surface and then raised to illuminate detail in shadows.

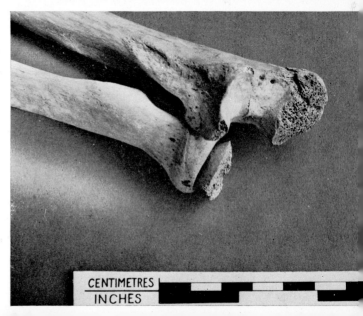

25

Latin manuscript on parchment. Photographed with Gandolfi 5×4 field camera, 203 mm lens.

In (a) the writing does not stand out at all well from the background and is much obscured by dirt and blots, which show in much greater contrast: aperture ƒ.32, Ilford FP3 film; lighting two 150 watt bulbs in reflectors two feet away at 45 degrees; 10 seconds exposure. Developed in Kodak Time Standard Developer for 10 minutes.

(b) Though the blemishes are undiminished the text stands out in much improved contrast and is for the most part clearly legible (to a scholar with the necessary linguistic equipment!). Aperture ƒ.22, 2B filter, 10 seconds exposure recommended for ultraviolet fluorescence Kodak Ortho Royal film: lighting two ultraviolet lamps 2 feet away at 45 degrees. The writing fluoresced strongly. Developed in Kodak Time Standard Developer for 20 minutes, twice normal developing time.

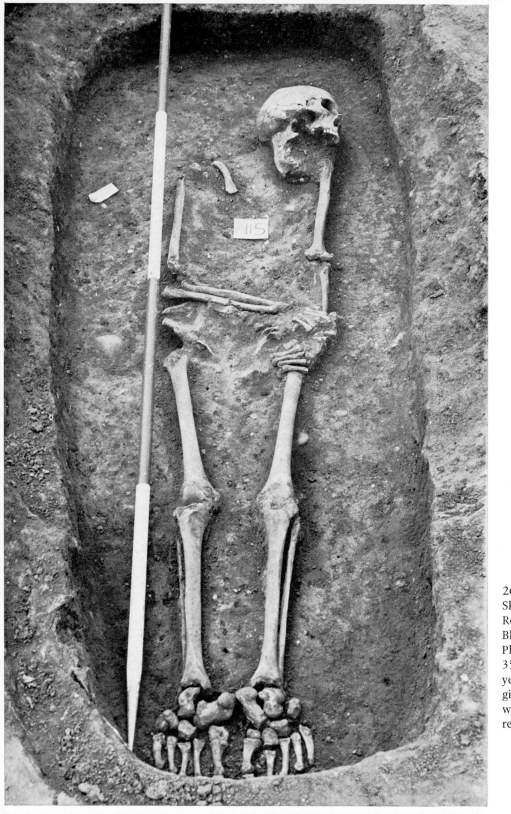

26
Skeleton from a late Roman cemetery at Bletsoe, Bedfordshire. Photographed with a 35 mm camera using a yellow-green filter to give contrast. FP4 film with a Weston meter reading. (C. Colyer)

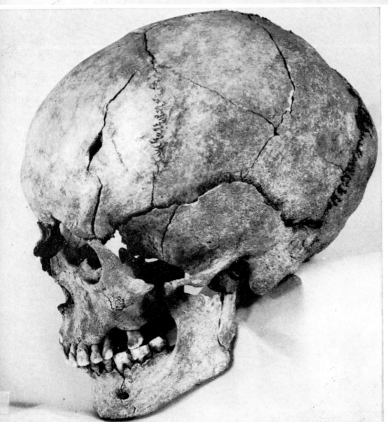

27
Fragments of skull. These were photographed as a group at an early stage of reconstruction. Some artificial light was added to pick up detail otherwise in shadow. The 5×4 camera was used with a 6½ inch lens, panchromatic film aperture ƒ.22.

28
The completed skull reconstruction photographed as for 27 but with aperture ƒ.45 and yellow-green filter for contrast. Two 150 watt lamps in reflector were placed, one top side, one lighting heavier detail of the front jaw.

29
Verulamium mosaic.
(a) the picture shows good contrast and even overall illumination; photographed on $8\frac{1}{2} \times 6\frac{1}{2}$ plate.

(b) The light on the mosaic is slightly uneven but the floor and walls are clearly separated, with the light coming towards the camera viewpoint, giving the necessary detail in the shadow (M. B. Cookson)

30 Photoplanning. For the accurate location of reference points a high viewpoint is essential. A camera-mount such as that illustrated may be improvised on the site, constructed in this case of bolted lightweight Dexion angle carefully designed with oblique wire stays to give the necessary rigidity. It is 30 feet high and covers an area of 5 m square, suitable for coverage by a 35 mm camera using the 50 mm lens. The camera was hauled into position by a cord passing over a pulley near the apex of the 'pyramid' and a cable-release, approximately 35 feet long, was first used to trip the shutter. Later this was replaced by an electronic release. Reference points on the ground were marked by the intersections of large (9″) wooden crosses, the arms of which were painted black and white for easy identification. The results were of satisfactory accuracy.

31 Hebrides.
(a) Oblique lighting towards the camera position throws the post-holes and empty stone-holes into shadow, while making the surrounding foundations stand out in pronounced relief.

(b) From a second viewpoint the oblique side-light still shows the post-holes in shadow and brings out the detail in the stone foundations. Both photographs taken with Gandolfi 5×4 camera, 203 mm lens, panchromatic film, aperture ƒ.32, Weston meter reading ×3.

32 London Bridge. This well and its wooden lining was completely in shadow. It was lit by several flashes during a time exposure to bring out the necessary contrast, and to show the water standing in it. Photographed with Gandolfi 5×4 camera, 203 mm lens, panchromatic film, aperture ƒ.32, exposure 20 seconds.

33

(a) Wide-angle view of a trench—too near a viewpoint and the angle of the camera have caused unsharpness at the bottom of the trench, as well as the converging parallels. Photographed on $4\frac{1}{4}\times3\frac{1}{4}$ hand and stand camera, panchromatic film, aperture ƒ.22, exposure according to Weston meter reading.

(b) Wide-angle close-up view of stonework—photographed at rather too close quarters, But the attitude of the ranging pole and edges of trench were carefully chosen. $4\frac{1}{4}\times3\frac{1}{4}$ hand and stand camera, panchromatic film, yellow filter, aperture ƒ.22, Weston meter reading $\times3$.

34 Billingsgate, Roman baths. Taken with 5×4 camera, 4½ inch wide-angle lens, pancromatic film, aperture ƒ.32, 1½ minutes. Natural lighting—daylight softened by partly corrugated roof.

35 Showcase at the Guildhall Museum. Using a 35 mm camera with a wide-angle lens. A black cloth was held in front of the case in the camera position. The camera lens projected through a hole cut in the centre of the cloth. This technique is most successful for cutting out reflections of the camera operator or other irrelevancies. A wire running through the top hem of the cloth enables it to be hung in position if the photographer is single-handed.

36
Head of Serapis. This head, now in the Guildhall Museum, London, was photographed in daylight and black cloths were used behind the camera and at the side of the display case to cut out reflections. A 6 inch (150 mm) lens was used on a Gandolfi 5×4 field camera with FP4 film, exposure 60 seconds, developed in Kodak Time Standard Developer for 10 minutes at 68°F.

37
Victoria and Albert Museum.
Column with the Martyrdom of St
Stephen and allegorical carvings.
Walnut. 35 mm camera, 135 tele-
photo lens FP4 film, 20 seconds.
Electronic flashes during the time
exposure gave the detail which was
dark and very much in shadow.

38   The Neptune Dish. Photographed with a 35 mm camera using the 50 mm lens, aperture *f*.56, exposure 1/30th second, with hand-held camera, as tripods are not allowed in the British Museum; developed in Kodak D76 developer 1–1 for 10 minutes; a soft result was obtained to get the required contrast in the enlarging; the position was chosen so that reflections from the glass top and sides of the display cabinet were minimal.

39   East window of Christ Church, Woburn Square. Gandolfi 5×4 field camera, 203 mm lens, panchromatic film. (a) Weston meter reading 40 seconds ƒ.32. Normal 10 minutes development in Kodak Time Standard Developer. Strong light through the window gives excessive contrast with some loss of detail. (b) Exposed for ×3 Weston meter reading: 2 minutes ƒ.32. Developed for 4 minutes in Kodak Time Standard Developer. This produces a soft negative that can be controlled in printing, with much less contrast than by normal treatment. (A. Shishtani)

40
(a) and (b). When the camera is tilted upwards parallels tend to slope towards each other as in (b). This is particularly a fault of the non-adjustable 35 mm camera. Cameras with the rising and tilting front panel, and swing back, enable distortion to be corrected by raising the lens-panel to include the higher parts of the subject, or in extreme cases by tilting the front panel; this means using the swing back to correct focus. (K. Fielding)

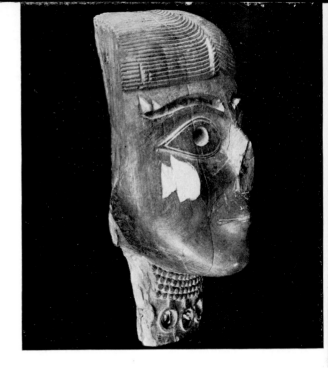

41
Ivory head of a lady from a well in the north-west palace at Nimrud, Iraq. These three positions, front (a), side (b) and back (c), were photographed with a Kodak half-plate specialised camera and panchromatic film. The object was raised away from the background with blocks of plasticine to give a sharp outline. Using a 150 watt lamp in a reflector, the light was moved about to show up the modelling and render the texture of the ivory. The studded collar in which jewels may once have been mounted stands out in clear relief. Displayed at the Metropolitan Museum, New York. (British School of Archaeology in Iraq.)

CENTIMETRES
INCHES

42 Seal impressions in modelling wax. (a) The deep-cut engraving of these impressions casts heavy shadows when an oblique light is used to show up the details. Photographed on the 5×4 camera, 6½ inch lens, aperture ƒ.45, panchromatic film. Lighting by one 150 watt lamp in reflector, moving this about to relieve the deeper shadows. (b) Using the same 5×4 camera with 6½ inch lens, panchromatic film, aperture ƒ.32, exposure 1/25th second; a synchronised flash was fired from just above the lens position and gives a slightly softer effect. All detail is visible.

CENTIMETRES
INCHES

43
Columbian seed beads. Objects were laid on perspex mounted on two supports with white paper draped underneath. A single 150 watt lamp in its reflector was kept moving during a time exposure of 15 seconds at aperture f.32. Panchromatic film, 5×4 format. This lighting eliminated all back-shadows, retaining the outlines and surface detail.

44
Iron Age pot from Meare, Somerset. Though the object lacks pictorial interest it was made to appear more attractive by carefully designed lighting. One lamp above and slightly to one side lit the rim and one side. A second lamp slightly above the centre on the side of the incised ornament gave added roundness and picked out the pattern. The hand and stand camera was used, 4¼×3¼ format, panchromatic film, aperture f.32, exposure calculated by meter reading ×2. Developed in Kodak Time Standard Developer for eight minutes. The print was made on contrasty paper.

45

(a) Bronze Age pottery urn from a cremated burial at Haverfordwest, Pembrokeshire. Photographed on half-plate camera, panchromatic film, aperture *f*.45, to ensure a sharp image. The pot was laid horizontally on two blocks of wood, raising it above a black cloth. This ensured clear separation from the background for if the pot had been laid directly on the cloth the outline would have appeared weak. The mouth-end of the pot was raised slightly higher so that the whole of the mouth and rim could be seen. Lighting was artificial, from the mouth-end of the pot, with a small relief lamp to show the lower part of the decoration. Without this the part below the deep rim would have been in too heavy shadow.

(b) Palestinian storage jar, sixth to fifth century B.C. The same technique was used in this photograph. The pointed base shows up well as do the handles and rim. A black cloth was placed under the subject to give contrast.

CENTIMETRES

CENTIMETRES

INCHES

46   Cylinder seal and its plasticine impression. The 5×4 field camera was used with a $4\frac{1}{4}$ inch lens by means of which, with the necessary bellows extension, a close-up view was obtained showing all necessary detail. The small hand-lamp was carefully manipulated in an oblique position, moving it about, watching the design, and penetrating the shadows. An aperture of ƒ.32 was used to ensure a sharp image since the plane of the thin, flat impression was more than $\frac{1}{2}$ inch below that of the summit of the cylinder.

47 Woven mat impressions on pottery. Photographed with the $4\frac{1}{4}\times3\frac{1}{4}$ hand and stand camera, panchromatic film, aperture f.22, Kodak Time Standard Developer. (a) Although some detail of the pattern on these fragments showed, the lighting was flat. (b) Oblique lighting with a moving 150 watt lamp in reflector, holding the lamp two-thirds of the time in a low position, then above for overall shadow detail.

48
Rendering of fine detail on silver. An oblique strong light was diffused by passing it through fibreglass fabric. The engraving showed up well, but the diffused light resulted in a soft general effect, so that contrast could be controlled in the printing. Orthochromatic film, 5×4 format, 203 mm lens, aperture *f*.32, exposure 10 seconds, developed in Kodak Time Standard Developer for 7 minutes.

49
Leaf impression in travertine. Using 5×4 format, 203 mm lens Ilford N50 process film, aperture *f*.22. The detail required being black and the background neutral, the subject lent itself to the process treatment for reproduction. Developed in Ilford Universal Developer to avoid too much contrast. It is advisable in such a case to over-expose ×2 or ×3 to produce a softer negative, reducing the developing time, and controlling the eventual contrast in the enlarging.

50

Coins obverse and reverse. This technique requires a black background. For changing to the reverse side the coins can be kept in line by placing a small spot in the position where they are to be placed. All details on pages 81–2.

51

Gold medals. Solid gold medals, so lighted obliquely that the raised design appears in sharp contrast against the lower background surface. The 5×4 format was used loaded with FP4 film. A polarising filter was fitted, and the lighting was by diffused natural daylight. The black background enhances the appearance of gold. Negatives were kept soft by controlled developing time, enabling the degrees of contrast needed to be obtained by choice of an appropriate grade of paper for the enlargement.

52 (a) Horsebit with dendritic structure. Using Exa 35 mm camera with 50 mm lens at an aperture of *f*.16, Ilford FP3 film, Unitol fine grain developer. One 150 watt lamp in reflector on one side to give a sharp edge pattern without too much shadow detail. A small piece of white card opposite the lamp picked up enough light to reflect into the shadows.
(b) Dendritic structure. The detailed area was photographed by the same method but extension tubes were used to give a degree of magnification on the negative suitable for further enlargement.

53 Flint knife with 'corn gloss' on the working edge and flaked flint axe-head. The black background is ideal to show contrast with the pale stone. The objects were mounted on plasticine chocks quite ½-inch above the background to give maximum definition of outlines. 5×4 format, panchromatic film, aperture ƒ.32, lighting by one 150 watt lamp in its reflector. This was moved upwards and downwards obliquely during a time exposure to pick out the relief and also for general illumination. Full exposure followed by slight under-development resulted in a soft negative enabling control of contrast to be exerted during printing.

55 (a) The Post Office tower, London, in early morning mist. Camera 5×4 field, 203 mm lens, aperture ƒ.32, panchromatic film, 1 second.

(b) Same time as (a). 3 seconds, 88A filter, Kodak infrared plate, developed in Kodak Time Standard Developer for 10 minutes.

Opposite:

54 Silbury. (a) View of Silbury Hill, Wiltshire, taken with Gandolfi 5×4 camera, 203 mm lens, panchromatic film, aperture ƒ.32, 1 second; weak midday sun, haze.
(b) View and time of day as (a). Kodak infrared plate, 88A filter, aperture ƒ.32, 6 seconds. Infrared radiation instead of the visible part of the spectrum penetrates the haze, showing details on the horizon invisible to the panchromatic material used for (a).

56　(a) View from the roof of the Institute of Archaeology. The camera used was the 5×4 with a 203 mm lens. Panchromatic film, aperture ƒ.32, exposure 1 second. Photographed in mid-morning, heavy mist, but strong sun above.

(b) View through mist by infrared. The buildings, warmed by the sun, are emitting plentiful infrared secondary radiation, to which the mist is transparent. The used of a small aperture is necessary to ensure focusing correction in the lens, designed for the visible part of the spectrum not the infra-red. Kodak infrared plate, 88A filter, aperture ƒ.32, 3 seconds exposure.

57

(a) St Pauls and Thames-side scene, with early morning mist. 35 mm camera, 50 mm lens, FP4 film, developed in Unitol Fine Grain Developer. Exposure according to meter reading Weston 125.

(b) 35 mm camera, 50 mm lens, aperture ƒ.22. Kodak infrared film using an 88A filter. Developed in Kodak D76 Developer diluted 1–3 instead of 1–1 as formula. Building the development up slowly minimises the grain.

(c) 35 mm camera, 135 mm tele-photo lens, 88A filter, Kodak infra-red film. Developed as (b).

58
Sherds. Using the 5×4 camera, 203 mm lens, two 500 photoflood lamps at 45 degrees;
(a) panchromatic film, exposure 8 seconds, ƒ.32. Developed in Kodak Time Standard Developer, at 68°F for 10 minutes. Ordinary light accentuates the (irrelevant) relief of the sherds and, in monochrome, it is scarcely appreciable that they are painted.

(b) 88A filter, Kodak infrared plate, exposure 20 seconds, ƒ.32. Developed in Kodak Time Standard Developer, at 68°F for 10 minutes. Reflected infrared, from the same sources as in (a), shows up the painted areas in good contrast with their background and plays down surface irregularities.

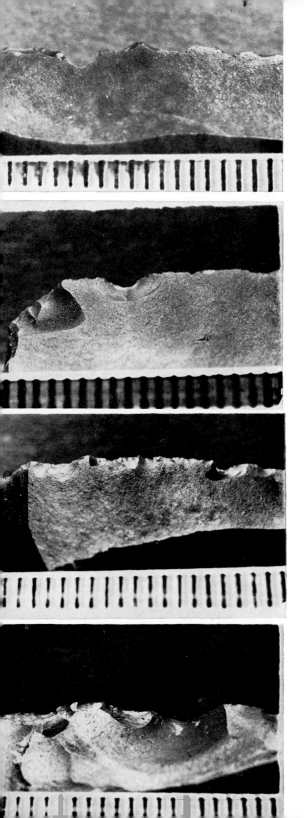

59

Cutting edges of flint tools. (a) Using the 35 mm camera with bellows extension and 50 mm lens, Pan F film, ƒ.16, Unitol Developer. The background is too similar in tone to render the outline of the cutting edge. Lighting is too soft also. Scale in mm.

(b), (c) and (d) Using the 35 mm camera, 50 mm lens and bellows extension; aperture ƒ.16, Pan F film, Unitol Developer. The darker background with strong oblique light from a microscope lamp gave this the required clean detail in each case. The scale is in millimetres in each case.

60
(a) and (b) Macrophotograph of a beetle. Daylight illumination was used to reduce the inevitably high contrast on the shiny armour. The 50 mm lens was fitted onto the 35 mm bellows extension. Aperture ƒ.16, 10 seconds exposure. Developed in Unitol Fine Grain Developer for 10 minutes at 68°F. Scale: cms. (c) Close-up of beetle's head. As (a), using higher magnification by extending the bellows. Scale: mm.

61
Medieval burial shroud. A series of photographs taken of a burial shroud and various pieces—beetles, bone and crystals—found with it. The shroud, composed mostly of wool, was found in a limestone sarcophagus of circa A.D. 1200 in the church of St Peter, Oxford.

(a) Detail showing the iron cross. Two photoflood 500 watt lamps were used to cover evenly the shroud without losing the variation of tone and colour. A Gandolfi 5×4 in. field camera was used with Kodak infrared 5×4 plate, 88A filter, aperture ƒ.32, developed in Kodak Time Standard Developer for 10 minutes at 68°F.

(b) Microphotograph of secondary crystal deposit found on bone and on the shroud (×60). The light source was one 200 watt lamp using a 35 mm camera, developed in Unitol Fine Grain Developer for 10 minutes.

61

(c) Microphotograph of cancellous bone tissue (×45). Photographed using polarized light; 35 mm camera, developed in Unitol Fine Grain Developer for 10 minutes at 68°F.

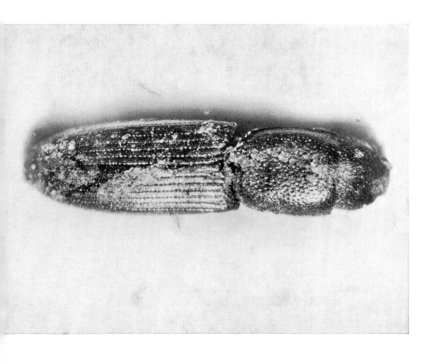

61

(d) Microphotograph of a beetle found with the shroud (×36). Photographed using polarized light, 35 mm camera, developed in Unitol Fine Grain Developer for 10 minutes at 68°F.

62

(a) This wrought-iron cannon ball was photographed with the 35 mm camera and 50 mm lens. Artificial lighting was used to show some detail. FP4 film, aperture $f.22$, exposure as meter reading, Unitol Fine Grain Developer, printed on contrasting paper to emphasize the relief.

(b) The iron of the cannon ball was 'sweating' (actively corroding). This was due to the chlorides contained picking up moisture from too humid atmosphere. Photographed under the microscope by daylight. Heat from any lamp used would have evaporated the moisture. The daylight was strong and fell obliquely on the subject. 3·5 objective, ×6 ocular, FP4 film, developed in Unitol Fine Grain Developer.

63

Leitz microscope. An old research-microscope in good condition, procured at a very reasonable cost. It is especially valuable for the long rack on the tube which gives much more working-space above the stage, either for low-power photo-micrography down to ×10 or for episcopic work, by reflected incident light, on relatively thick objects such as potsherds or seals. The many refinements make for great flexibility using transmitted light: centring substage and iris with filter-tray; swing-out Abbé condenser with its own iris; stage; revolving and centring with mechanical slide-holders and micrometers; tube; standard length with 100 mm draw tube, fitted with three-way revolving nose-piece; camera-adaptor as for Prior microscope; rough focusing by rackwork; fine adjustment on pillar; variety of available objectives and oculars.

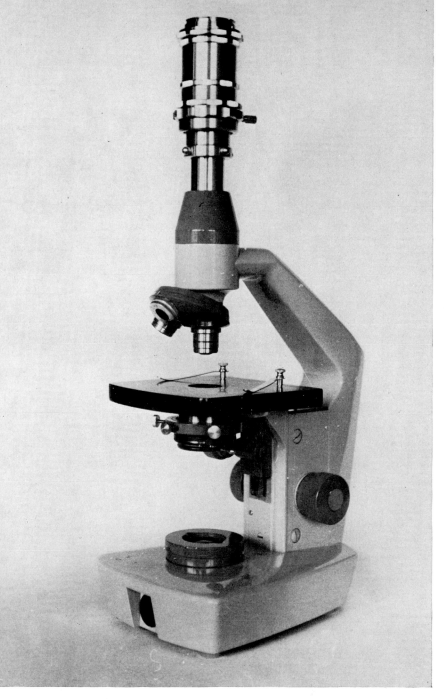

64

Prior microscope. A fixed-limb student's microscope with focusing stage and built-in substage lighting. Fitted with objectives $\times 3\cdot 5$, $\times 6$ and $\times 10$ in triple nose-piece; oculars $\times 6$ and $\times 10$. Abbé substage condenser and iris in centring ring. For photography, a mount to carry the camera at the ocular is permanently fitted and a choice of extension-rings may be used as shown to increase magnification as desired.

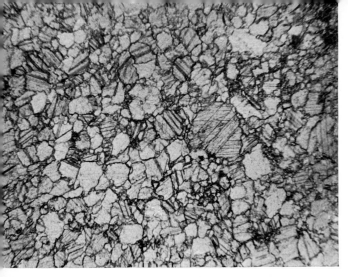

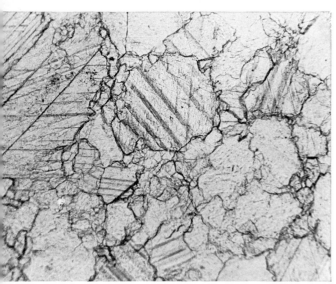

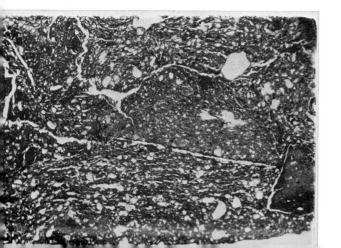

65

(a) Prior photomicrograph. Thin-section of crystalline igneous rock, in transmitted plane-polarised light. Lamellar twinning of felspar crystals and their cleavages give banded and hatched effects. 3·5 objective, ×5 ocular, polarised light transmitted 60 seconds.

(b) Higher magnification, ×10 objective, ×5 ocular. Polarised light transmitted.

(c) Prior photomicrograph. Thin-section of prehistoric pottery containing 'grog' (crushed potsherds) as filler. The angular fragments of different texture stand out well from their matrix of moulded clay, the latter showing flow-structures. ×3·5 objective, ×10 ocular, transmitted light, 15 seconds exposure.

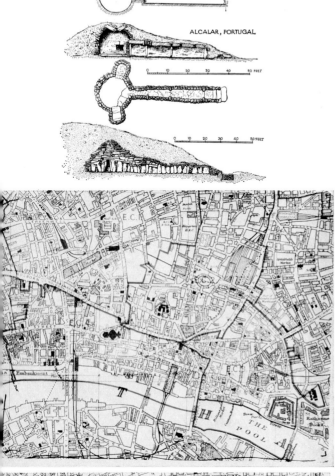

TREASURY OF ATREUS, MYCENAE, GREECE

ALCALAR, PORTUGAL

(a) Line drawing. In making a line block for publishing a high quality print is most essential. Every line, coarse or fine, of the original drawing must be shown distinctly. The print for the block-maker should be of medium contrast. This drawing was photographed on a quarter-plate negative, with the use of a copying camera, using a process lens $f.16$. The camera has a negative carrier for the use of $3\frac{1}{2} \times 2\frac{1}{2}$ to $8\frac{1}{2} \times 6\frac{1}{2}$, the lens of multiple extension, 10 inch focal length, covers all formats. It has bellows for higher magnification. Process film was used for this negative and Kodak Time Standard Developer to prevent too much contrast. This is controlled in the printing.

(b) Map with red lines to be eliminated. Photographed on half-plate negative using panchromatic film, aperture $f.32$. Developed in Ilford Universal Developer. The lines delimiting the London postal districts and the lettering (EC1, EC2, EC3 etc) are not wanted on the eventual print. They are printed in red on the original.

(c) Map with red detail lines eliminated. Photographed on half-plate negative using panchromatic film and red filter to eliminate red lines. Aperture $f.32$. Developed in Ilford Universal Developer.

67

Example of screens for blocks

(a) Original fine-screen half-tone illustration from book.

(b) (*opposite*) Part of the same, magnified ×7.

(c) (*opposite*) Part of the same, magnified ×60.

Coarse screen for newspaper half-tones

67

(d) Part of newspaper illustration.

(e) Newspaper ×9.

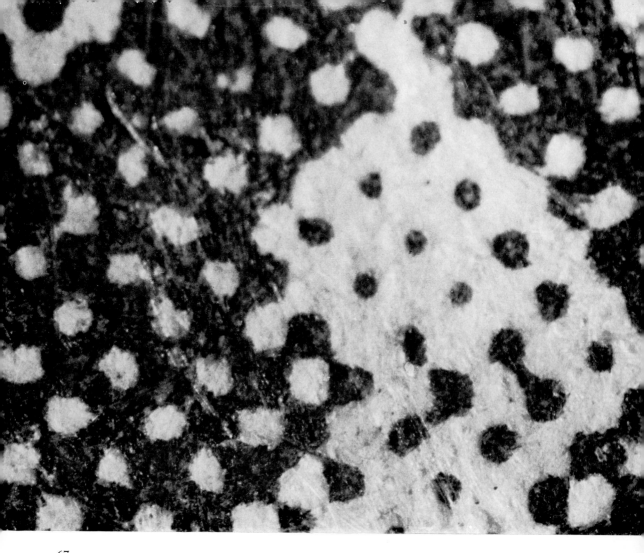

67
(f) Newspaper ×60.

Index

Index